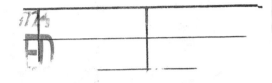

The Craft Industries

Geraint Jenkins

Longman

LONGMAN GROUP LIMITED
London

Associated companies, branches and representatives
throughout the world

© *Geraint Jenkins* 1972

First published 1972

ISBN 0 582 12796 3

Printed in Great Britain
by W & J Mackay Limited, Chatham

164.034

B/965-6

Contents

List of Illustrations

vii

Sources of Illustrations

The author and publishers wish to thank the following for permission to use photographs: Miss M. White for Nos 1, 2, 3, 7, 8; Museum of English Rural Life, University of Reading for Nos 4, 20; Welsh Folk Museum, National Museum of Wales for Nos 5, 6, 12, 13, 14, 18; D. J. Stanbury for No 9; The Radio Times Hulton Picture Library for Nos 10, 21; The Leather Institute for Nos 15, 16; J. H. Thornton for No 17; C. F. Snow for No 19; Sheffield City Museums for Nos 22, 23; Dudley Museum for Nos 24–29; No 11 is from the author's collection.

Line Drawings in the Text

Acknowledgements

The author wishes to thank the following for help in preparing this book: Mrs Anna Meredith, City Museum, Birmingham; Mr R. S. G. Traves, Museum and Art Gallery, Dudley; Mr A. C. Sanctuary, Bridport; the Borough Librarian, Public Library, Redditch; Miss M. E. Samuel, Dorchester Museum. He is also grateful to Mr S. F. Sanderson of the School of English, University of Leeds, for allowing him to consult manuscripts in the Archives of the Institute of Dialect and Folk Life Studies and to make use of the work of the following, deposited at the Institute: Miss V. A. Napier, Miss E. K. Hawley, Mr K. Atkin and Mr E. J. Penny. He owes a special debt of gratitude to a large number of craftsmen who gave him access to their premises and gave freely of their time and knowledge to answer questions.

Introduction

Until fairly recent times every community in the land was largely self sufficient and only on rare occasions did the inhabitants of rural Britain, in particular, venture far outside their own communities to search for the means of life. A large proportion of the population were born, lived and died within the narrow confines of their own localities, and most realised their ambitions within their own communities, to which they were tied by ties of blood, family and neighbourliness.

During this period of near economic self-sufficiency, craft workshops were numerous and important, while domestic crafts such as beer brewing, butter and cheese making, malting and many others were widely practised. The products of the farm—corn, animal skins and wool—could always be taken to a nearby mill for processing; the products of those mills, for example cloth, tweeds and leather, could, in turn, be used by one of the many craftsmen of a neighbourhood to make some essential. Other products, such as flour, oatmeal and blankets, could be used directly in the home. In many cases the craftsmen who processed farm produce were not paid in cash, but were allowed to keep a proportion of the produce that a farmer brought in. Corn millers were allowed to keep a proportion of a farmer's quota of corn for their own use, while woollen manufacturers were allowed to keep a proportion of the fleeces brought in for making into yarn or blankets.

The processing crafts of Britain, where the craftsman was concerned with processing some raw material, usually demanded a range of immovable equipment and often required water power. For this reason the processing industries were more often than not practised in small factories or mills. Two buildings, a woollen mill and a country tannery at the Welsh Folk Museum, St Fagans, near Cardiff, required both water power and a wide range of heavy equipment.

The Esgair Moel Mill from Llanwrtyd, Brecknockshire, had the following equipment when it was dismantled for re-erection at the Museum in 1951:

A pair of dyeing vats, one equipped with a windlass.
Devil for intermixing and disentangling wool.
A scribbler carder with intermediate feed and carding engine with condenser.
Spinning mule of 80 spindles.
Twister.
Warping frame.
3 Hand looms.
Cutting machine.
Press.
Fulling stocks.
Rowing frame.
Tenter frame.

The Rhaeadr tannery is equipped with:

A water driven mill wheel and a mill for grinding bark.
A plentiful supply of clean water for initial washing of hides in a water pit 7 feet deep.
Three lime pits for initial immersion of hides before fleshing and unhairing.
Three mastering pits containing a mixture of hen or pigeon manure or dog dung and water for treating calf skins.
A pit for fleshings and other waste products.
Fifty tan pits containing oak bark and water in varying strengths for the actual tanning of hides.
Beams to act as work benches for fleshing and unhairing.
Unhairing and fleshing knives and scudding knives for removal of lime.
A wooden rounding table and knives for cutting up hides, into six or eight parts before tanning.
Hooks and long handled tongs for handling hides in pits; plungers for mixing oak bark, bark baskets and bark barrows.
A heavy brass roller for rolling tanned hides on a zinc rolling platform.
Horses and staking pins for removing wrinkles from tanned hides.

After rolling and striking, sole leather did not require further treatment before it could be used, but harness and boot upper leather had to be dressed by the currier. The currier's craft did not depend on water power or on any large, complex pieces of equipment, but on dexterity in the use of hand tools. Nevertheless, it was an advantage for the currier to locate his workshop either in or near the source of supply—the local tannery.

In addition to processing locally produced raw materials, every village, town and neighbourhood in the land had its craftsmen responsible for providing the tools, utensils and equipment required by the local community. Essentials ranging from field gates to footwear and from ploughs to shovels were produced by craftsmen who were primarily concerned with supplying a local market. Since each craftsman was responsible for producing essentials for his own district, he made those essentials according to local conditions of soil and topography, as well as the ingrained traditions of the various districts.

Despite the disappearance of a large proportion of the craft industries responsible for meeting a local or regional demand, it is interesting to note that even the products of modern industry are often based on designs that have remained unchanged for centuries.

In some fields of modern production, standardisation has not progressed as far as one would have expected. Modern tool catalogues show a vast range of tools and implements, ranging from currier's knives to mason's cockscombs, and from farrier's hoof parers to sugar nippers, the design of which has not changed to any extent in hundreds of years, and that could well fit into a museum's representation of eighteenth-century craft workshops. Mass production has failed to standardise the types of tool and implement used by craftsmen and land workers at the present time, and any manufacturer concerned with supplying their needs must pay due attention both to the ingrained traditions of localities and to the conservatism of many trades. Attention must be paid, too, to the specific needs of regions from the point of view of topography, soil and vegetation. For example, in the nineteenth century, Ransome, the well-known East Anglian manufacturer of farm implements, realised the importance of these factors, and in producing ploughs, his firm produced a great variety of mouldboard and share, based on the multiplicity of regional design. In the 1860s and 70s, Ransome employed a team of horses and a skilled ploughman to take part in ploughing matches throughout the country, and in this way they learned of local needs by practical experience.

When village craftsmen were concerned with tools and implements for their own localities, they took into full consideration such factors as soil and vegetation as well as the traditions of the localities. Thus a wheelwright in the Vale of Berkeley, for example, made wagons that were well adapted to the natural conditions of the Vale.[1] He provided his blue painted wagons with greatly dished double-straked wheels as befitted a clay land district; he provided them with tall nearly upright fore and tail ladders to carry the heavy hay crops of this dairying region, and since the roads and lanes of the district are generally straight the locking capacity of the wagon was not a first consideration. The yellow-painted Cotswold wagons, on the other hand, were entirely different. Here, the wheelwrights built their wagons as light as possible, as befitted a region with many abrupt changes of slope. Lock was extremely important and small, nearly horizontal fore and tail ladders were fitted. These were designed to carry corn sheaves rather than hay and the whole vehicle was designed for a rolling countryside where sheep raising and cereal growing formed the basis of the economy.

But local designs, adapted to the needs of various localities of Britain could not only be seen in ploughs, wagons, harrows and other large implements. They were also displayed in the variety of hand tools made by country craftsmen. Estyn Evans in describing the Irish spade, for example, states:

> The precise requirements of each group of townlands forming a neighbourhood unit, resulted from the balance of many physical, human and economic factors—such as conditions of soil and slope, e.g. methods of digging, types of crop, length of arm and leg— cemented by usage and sanctioned by tradition. The 'spade gauge book' of a County Tyrone factory, which has recently closed, lists some 230 different patterns . . . and it served only Ulster and the West.[2]

A tool that varied greatly from district to district was the billhook, a tool described by Richard Jeffreys as 'the national weapon of the English labourer'. In the past, billhooks, like other farm tools, were made by village blacksmiths for the farming population of their own immediate districts and, since each tool was designed for dealing with a specific type of vegetation and local conditions, many hundreds of different types must have existed. Not only did the shape and size of blade vary tremendously, but the distribution of weight in each tool also varied, as did the shape of the handle. On the Suffolk coast, for example, billhooks made by craftsmen in such places as Orford and Woodbridge were designed primarily for cutting edges and banks mainly below the level of the worker. Consequently the blades were heavier at the front and each tool was equipped with a fairly long round handle. To deal with rough sedge and rushes as well as woody roots, the Suffolk billhook had a slightly convex blade with a short straight bite at the end for dealing with those roots. The billhooks of Brecknockshire, on the other hand, were designed primarily for laying hedges of straight hazel, willow and thorn, and consequently the pistol-handled tool required had an almost straight blade. Leicester billhooks were wide and therefore their blades were made much thinner to cut down the weight. Each tool had two blades; the one sharply curved almost to a sickle shape to cut the lush vegetation of its district, whilst the other at the back was straight and was used to cut the thorn tufts occasionally found on the grassy banks of the Midlands.

The shape of the handle and the method of hafting also varied considerably from district to district. In some places such as West Carmarthenshire, where briar and thorn predominate, long turned handles which kept the worker's hand well clear of the prickles were preferred, while in many other districts, such as Oxfordshire, the billhooks were equipped with caulked or pistol-shaped handles. While most varieties were fitted to handles by tangs and metal ferrules, some billhooks were socketed and the rounded projection at the back of each blade was nailed to the handle. This was particularly important in billhooks such as the Suffolk, where the type of vegetation demanded a long cutting edge that could be continued as close to the handle as possible.

In addition to the regional styles of general purpose billhook, there were also those designed for a specific trade. For example, the wattle hurdle maker required two types of billhook. First he required a small sharply curving hurdling bill, designed specifically for splitting hazel rods, perhaps no more than 2 inches in diameter. Hurdling bills again varied from district to district, and those used by Dorset

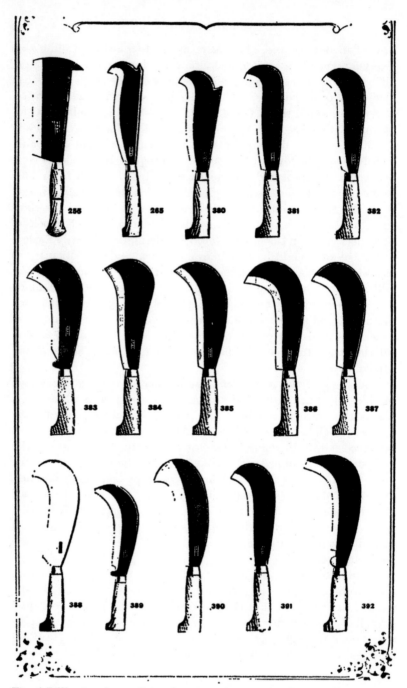

Fig. 1 Billhooks of a traditional pattern from the trade catalogue of Isaac Nash, 1899

craftsmen differed in detail from those used by Hampshire and Berkshire wattle hurdle makers. In addition the hurdle maker required a specially adapted bill with a concave blade ending in a cutting edge some 3 inches wide. To trim a finished hurdle, a short cudgel was thrust under the end to be trimmed and with a sharp blow of the billhook, the projecting rod was cleanly cut. Another specialised hook, which again varied from district to district, was the Spar hook. This had a concave cutting edge no more than 7 inches long and was specially designed for cleaving and trimming thatching spars.

In the nineteenth century, particularly during the last quarter, village craftsmen who supplied a distinctly local market with all its requirements were disappearing rapidly. Blacksmiths in particular ceased to be the essential craftsmen that they had been from time immemorial, for their work was being taken over by large-scale manufacturers in Yorkshire and the Midlands. Representatives of these manufacturers travelled widely and supplied ironmongers in market towns and villages with their products. In small farm tools they did not produce standardised products but clung to traditional local patterns and still maintained the old local names. One trade catalogue dating from 1900 states: 'We show only those patterns that are most generally used in their various districts. We do, however, still make any pattern hook and if the pattern which customers have been in the habit of buying is not shown here, we shall be pleased to supply them.'

While on the one hand, manufacturers have been adding to their range of patterns throughout the present century, on the other hand some patterns have disappeared and some measure of standardisation has been attempted. For example, Nash's 1899 catalogue does not show the Aberaeron billhook amongst its range of products, for at that period the well-known smithy in the Cardiganshire seaside town was flourishing and its socketed billhook with an oddly shaped projection at the back was in constant demand among the farmers of West Wales. When the smith stopped making billhooks in the 1920s, the pattern was taken over by Brades, Nash and Tyzack and appears as the 'Aberayron Billhook' in their recent catalogues. On the other hand, patterns such as the wide and clumsy Machynlleth billhook have gone out of production and its place taken by the well-known Newtown pattern, whose design can be traced back to a type made by village blacksmiths throughout North Wales.

Any measure of standardisation is therefore a very slow process. Mr F. H. Middleton, then Sales Director of Edward Elwell Ltd, Wednesbury, writes in a letter of 5 March 1964:

> We continue to manufacture the different types as the traditional demand is still very strong. If we tried to sell a Kent billhook in your part of the world, we doubt if we should succeed. On the other hand, there are one or two patterns, such as the Newtown and Stafford billhooks, that sell in many parts of the country. It might be an excellent idea to attempt standardisation and undoubtedly we shall have to do this in due time, but quite frankly there is an inherent danger in trying to force something upon people that differs from what they have normally purchased. Whilst we have a strong hold on this market, this should never be taken for granted as any refusal to supply might bring competition back again.

It may be added that ironmongers in Wales and the West of England have said that they would find it impossible to sell any other than the local pattern, and it may be suggested that variety has been preserved not only by the stability of local needs but by the conservatism of the countryman. The rural worker still insists on the familiar tool of his neighbourhood and large-scale manufacturers will not, perhaps dare not, introduce a standardised tool. Custom and tradition has dictated that a particular type of tool is best for a particular region and persistence in billhook design provides an excellent example of the persistence of ancient tradition in a most unexpected context.

Many of the industries that had their beginnings in small local craft workshops have developed into industries of considerable national importance. Many of them have developed because of the presence of the raw materials in the locality where they were first practised. The importance of High Wycombe as an important centre of furniture manufacture is in no small measure due to the existence of the beechwoods around it and to the primitive craftsmen that worked there.[3] The glove making industry carried out by women in their own homes in Somerset was based on the leather dressing industry in such towns as Yeovil,[4] while straw plaiting in Bedfordshire was based on the importance of corn growing in the economy of the East Midlands.[5]

In this work some of the more important craft industries practised in Britain in recent years are described. The industries described by no means provide a complete picture of all the craft industries that existed in Britain, many of which have been covered in other books in this series, but all those described here had their beginnings in small rural workshops, originally concerned with supplying a local or regional market. At some stage in the development of some of those craft industries, production went beyond the stage of supplying a strictly local market and the horizons of the craftsmen were widened to produce goods that were exported far beyond the confines of a locality.

CHAPTER ONE

Baskets

One of the oldest and certainly the most widespread craft industry is that of basket-making. In its essential characteristics it is one of the simplest arts, involving only the manipulation of rods. As there is such a vast variety of baskets, the craft has completely escaped the application of machinery and at all levels of culture it has remained a true handicraft and the process of weaving has changed in no important particular since prehistoric times.

The Somerset willow basket industry

For many centuries one of the main centres of the willow-growing and basket-making industry in Britain has been the Sedgemoor district of Somerset. Small ribbonlike villages such as Stathe, Burrow-bridge and Athelney provide the place of work for dozens of traditional craftsmen, while the flat marshy moors around the villages are extensively planted with willow, the basket-maker's raw material.

For the last fifteen miles or more of its course, the slow meandering river Parret is tidal, and during the winter months it often bursts its banks, inundating hundreds of acres of farmland. Fortunately the basket willow, varieties of the species *salix*, grows best on thick loamy soil, on land that is sometimes flooded, but at other times well drained. For this reason central Somerset has the ideal conditions for the osier growing and willow cultivation which, combined with a certain amount of livestock-rearing and dairying, provides the basis of the agricultural economy of this part of the country.

Much of the area between the Mendips and the Quantock Hills is divided into a large number of square plots or holts, each plot bounded on all sides not by fences or hedges but by wide ditches known as *rhines*. These ditches are primarily irrigation and drainage canals, but they are also widely used for carrying harvested willow, particularly in the winter months when the Parret is in flood.

There are countless varieties of basket willow, but the most common ones grown in Somerset are Black Maul and the heavy-cropping
Champion Rod varieties. Willow beds are replanted at infrequent
intervals; indeed there are beds in Athelney that still bear annual
crops of withy eighty years after planting. When a bed is planted the
ground has to be very thoroughly prepared; deep ploughing or
digging is essential. In the past steam ploughing tackle was widely
used, indeed some growers believed that the plough had to be followed
by a steam cultivator taken over the land at least eight times. If no
steam tackle was available the ground had to be dug by hand with a
spade to the depth of two spits. In present day Sedgemoor the ground is
ploughed with tractor ploughs in the autumn and winter months, but
before planting begins the plot has to be harrowed a number of times, all
the weeds are cleared by hand and the ground is thoroughly manured.

The willow grower purchases the best quality withy for cutting
into sets at one of the many auction sales held annually in a number
of Somerset villages. Regular auctions are held for example in the
village halls at Langport and North Curry in the autumn, and it is at
these auctions that local basket-makers as well as blind schools and
prisons obtain their raw material. The best quality rods are reserved
for planting and the growers' first task is to cut each rod into 12 or
15 inch sets. These are then placed in damp grass until the late
winter planting season begins.

With the bed fully prepared, the planter, armed with the sets,
begins the task of planting at the rate of between 18,000 and 24,000
sets to the acre. He pushes each set in with the palm of his right hand
until only some 7 inches of the set appears above the ground. Sets
are planted in rows, each being some 15 inches from the next, with
some 22 inches between each row. Willow sets grow very easily for
as the sap rises in the spring the buds in the soil form roots, while
those above ground grow very rapidly into the straight sticks that
will form the basket-maker's raw material.

During the early months of growth the withy beds have to be
hoed at frequent intervals and the crop sprayed with insecticides. In
the autumn the maiden crop of willow is harvested and although
this is rarely used, harvesting is nevertheless essential to ensure the
strengthening of the roots. It is only after three years that the willow
stool will bear a full crop of usable willow, usually at the rate of some
two or three tons of withy to the acre.

Harvesting is still carried out by hand, and throughout the autumn and winter months workers armed with simple harvesting hooks cut the rods as near the stool or stump as possible. A sharp upward movement of the hook is needed, to leave the cut ends as nearly vertical as possible so that the rain does not penetrate them. Good cutting is vital in willow harvesting for the stool has to bear a heavy crop of rods which have to be cut annually for many decades. After cutting, the rods have to be tied with willow bands into bundles known as *willow bed bundles* or *bolts*, each one measuring 3 feet 1 inch around the base. The average annual yield from an acre of willow is in the region of 100 bolts, weighing some three tons. These are transported, more often than not on flat-bottomed boats along the rhines to the basket-maker's workshop, to be used there or to be sold at the auction sales.

The length of life of a willow holt varies according to the suitability of the soil, the variety grown, and the care given to the crop. When the yield diminishes, the beds are let down to grass and the land grazed for four or five years before replanting with willow.

Although only two or three species of willow are grown in Somerset, the basket-maker uses three principal grades of raw material, each grade being known by its colour. These grades are obtained by the different treatment of the raw material after harvesting. All the willow in willow bed bundles is known as *green*. This is very rarely used nowadays although in the past it was used for making wattle hurdles and a cheap variety of basket. The main types used by basket-makers are brown, buff and white willow.

1. *Brown willow*. This is obtained by steaming sorted green rods in a steaming chest and then stacking them in the open to dry for many weeks. Brown willow is not stripped of its bark and green rods for browning may be cut at any time during the winter. Brown rods are widely used in Somerset for making wickerwork garden furniture as well as for making baskets for work exposed to damp, such as watercress baskets or those used in woollen factories.

2. *Buff willow*. To make buff rods, green willow after being sorted into foot size and again tied into bundles or *wads* is boiled vigorously for five hours and kept in the water for at least another twenty-four hours. The tannin in the bark stains the rods to a rich golden colour. The green rods, up to a hundred wads in number, are almost in-

variably placed in boiling water, but occasionally when the withy is very dry, green wads are placed in cold water which is brought to the boil. After being removed from the large rectangular boiler which usually measures 6 feet long, 5 feet wide and 4 feet deep, the boiled wads are stacked in heaps covered with willow bark, which in dry weather will be watered daily before the rods are ready for stripping.

3. *White willow.* Brown and buff willow may be obtained at any period of the year, preferably after green rods have been in store for at least six months, but white rods can be obtained only in the spring. Willow bed bundles that have been harvested in the autumn and winter are placed immediately in a few inches of running water in pits that have been especially designed for the purpose. They remain there until the spring. As the sap rises, the bundles of willow are removed and the bark stripped. In Somerset a large proportion of the baskets are made from white rods and as pitted willow can only be peeled between the beginning of April and the middle of June, whilst the sap is rising and the willows bursting into leaf, that period is usually one of feverish activity in the withy beds. A great deal of female labour is employed during these three months.

Products

Hundreds of different types of basket are made by rural basket-makers at the present time. Most of them are common throughout the country, others are only known in a limited region. The cran and swill, for example, are peculiar to the fish quays of Yarmouth and Lowestoft while the peck cob is known only to Suffolk farmers.[1] The products of rural basket-makers may, however, be divided into five distinct categories:

1. *Agricultural baskets* for use on farms. With the mechanisation of agriculture, these baskets are less common than they were twenty years ago. Examples of agricultural baskets are: potato pickers and the larger potato hampers formerly used for harvesting potatoes. Cattle feeding baskets and fruit picking baskets. Specialised local types are the broccoli crates of Cornwall, bushell baskets known as rips used on Sussex farms, and the stable skeps of the Newmarket district. Many Somerset craftsmen produce these baskets not only for the national but also for the regional markets.

2. *Market baskets* for transporting fruit, vegetables or other material to markets. Examples of this type are the bushel sieves of the Vale of Evesham; strikes for carrying 12 lb of tomatoes; flats for cucumbers; rim pecks for strawberries and chicken crates for carrying live birds.

3. *Industrial baskets*, for use in factories. Examples of this type are the Yorkshire skep, a square open basket some 3 feet high, often mounted on rollers and used in the textile mills; and hampers used in the Northamptonshire and the hosiery factories of Leicestershire.

4. *Trade baskets* for tradesmen's deliveries, such as laundry baskets and baker's baskets. The great variety of fish baskets, many of them with distinct local names come into this category as well. Examples of fish baskets are the prickle of Sussex, the cran and swill of Yarmouth and Lowestoft, the cockle flats of Ipswich and the salmon baskets made for Bristol fishmongers.

5. *Domestic and fancy baskets.* There are many varieties within this category ranging from barrel-shaped, buff shopping-baskets to highly-decorated needle-work baskets and from picnic baskets to kitten baskets.

In addition to actual osier receptacles made by rural craftsmen at the present time, most of them extend their activities to making wickerwork furniture and wattle hurdles. The rural craftsman faces intense competition at the present time, not only from such places as Hong Kong, Japan and Portugal, but also from Blind Institutions. This competition, more than any other factor, has caused the rural basket-maker to extend his activities into other related fields.

Processes

Despite the fact that there are hundreds of local and trade variations in basket design, the process of weaving is basically the same throughout the world. Before he begins a day's work, enough willow rods have been soaked overnight to make them pliable and easy to handle, and the basket-maker seated on the floor with a lap-board in front of him commences his task of weaving.

Whether a basket be round, square or oval, the base is almost invariably made first. If a rectangular or square basket is being made the rods are first of all fixed in a small slamp made of two wooden blocks clipped or bolted together and the finer rods woven between the upright sticks. If it is a round or oval basket, however, a start is made with the *slath*, which consists of a number of rods overlapping crosswise. They are bound together and spread out to radiate from the centre like the spokes of a wheel. Finer rods are interwoven between these radiating stakes, and if the basket is large, more stakes are inserted as the work proceeds to make the base perfectly strong. When the base is complete, the edge being reinforced with a stouter weave, extra rods are inserted and bent up to form the side frame. A willow hoop is made and passed around the upright stakes to keep them in place as the work proceeds. Finer rods are woven round the round between the upright stakes from left to right, each rod being cut at the butt and inserted in the weave to overlap the end of the previous rod. The long ends of the stakes are finally woven along the rim to form a firm edge.

There are a number of strokes, or complete movements analogous to a stitch in needlework that the basket-makers adopt. The principal ones are:

Randing. A single rod is worked alternately in front of and behind the upright stakes.

Slewing. Two or more rods are worked together alternately in front of and behind the upright stakes.

Fitching. The rods are worked alternately under and over each other, gripping a stake at each stroke. This process is mainly used in making skeleton baskets, such as poultry baskets. The distance between the stakes has to be judged very accurately.

Pairing. Two rods are worked alternately over and under each other —the reverse of a fitch.

Waling. Three or more rods are worked alternately one by one in front of two, three or more stakes and behind one. This is a stout weave often used to edge the bottom of the basket.

Upsett. Two, three or more rods of willow worked alternately on the stakes immediately they are pricked up from the base.

Although in most cases a basket is made from the bottom upwards there are exceptions to this rule. The well known Yarmouth swill for example is built from the rim downwards, as is the Southport boat (a market basket used by Lancashire countrywomen) and the Welsh gwyntell.

Tools and equipment

Brakes. These are used for stripping willow. Each one consists of two pieces of springy iron some 20 inches long set in an upright wooden frame, the iron blades being designed to pinch the willow rod as it is drawn between them. Women are often employed, particularly when peeling white withy in Somerset. The bark at the butt end of a withy rod is first loosened and the rod is then reversed and drawn right through the jaws leaving the bark behind.

Strippler. In some of the larger workshops, electrically-driven peeling machines or stripplers have been introduced in recent years. The strippler stands some 5 ft high and 2 ft 6 in wide and has the appearance of a winnowing-machine. A rapidly-revolving drum carries a series of scrapers and as the craftsman places a bundle of willow against this drum, drawing it backwards and forwards, the bark is completely removed.

Sorting equipment. The rods in a willow bed bundle are only roughly sorted to size before they are put into store. Before they can be used by the basket-maker they must be classified into foot sizes. A barrel is sunk in the ground and standing alongside it, the sorter places a bundle of rods in the barrel. With the help of a graduated stick he draws out the longest rods, each one being around 9 ft in length, and continues the process right down until the shortest 2 ft rods have been removed. The sorted heaps are then tied into bundles or wads, each wad being 37 inches in diameter at the bottom.

Cleaver. Although most of the white and buff rods are used in the natural round state, some are cut down to make finer material known as *skeins*. A little tool no more than four inches long, called a cleaver is passed down each rod. A slit is first cut in the butt of the rod and the cleaver, which has three or four radiating wooden, metal or bone cutting edges, is pushed down the length of the rod, cutting it into three or four portions. Cleavers may be all-wooden, all bone, or wooden handled with metal blades.

Shave. This is a small plane-like tool through which skeins are passed to shave off the inner pith, leaving a narrow, pliable band of timber. A shave has a wooden stock some 4 inches long and 2 inches wide, shod with metal. A small blade $1\frac{1}{2}$ inches wide is bolted to the stock and the skein is passed between the blade and the metal shoe; the whole tool being small enough for the basket-maker to hold it in the palm of his hand.

Upright. This is similar in size and shape to the shave, but it differs from it in that it has two parallel blades underneath the stock. It is used to reduce skeins to the same width throughout their length, by drawing each one between the blades. The width of skein can be adjusted by turning a small brass screw on top of the stock.

Lap board. The basket-maker sits on the floor with his back against the wall. His work bench is a wooden plank some 72 inches long and 30 inches wide, placed between his outstretched legs. If he wishes to raise the height of his basket, then a sloping table, known as a lap board, can be placed on the plank. This is some 35 inches long, 30 inches wide and stands 6 or 7 inches high at the back.

Bodkin. To make openings in the weave for the insertion of rods, the craftsman uses a wooden, iron or bone bodkin, which varies in length from as little as 3 inches to 10 inches.

Shop knife. This is a narrow bladed knife, usually some 7 inches long, for pointing willow rods before insertion. Some craftsmen use an ordinary penknife for this purpose.

Picking knife. This is a very short knife with a blade no more than 3 inches long for trimming finished baskets. It has a thick convex blade with a sharp point. It has hardly altered in shape over the centuries, for with the beating iron, it appears on Arms of the Company of Basketmakers established in 1569.

Beating iron or shop iron. This is a piece of iron approximately 9 inches long and 3 inches wide used by the basket-maker for beating the weave into place as the work progresses.

Commander. This consists of an iron rod, ringed at its tip for straightening the heavier stakes and also for beating the weave. The most common type measures some 9 inches in length.

In addition to these essential pieces of equipment, the basket-maker also needs a tank for soaking willow, a heavy weight for placing in the base of the basket while he weaves the sides, and a small pair of clippers or shears for cutting the thicker pieces of willow. In addition, some craftsmen have small horns containing grease in their workshops. A bodkin is dipped in this as it is far easier to use after greasing.

Willow basket-making is a craft that requires not only great dexterity but considerable strength, for willow, even after soaking in water, is difficult to bend and weave. But despite foreign competition, the craft in Somerset is still flourishing and the demand for traditional baskets is still high. The only cloud on the horizon is the fact that the industry is not attracting young people to its ranks. This is partly because basket-making is a craft that requires a five-year apprenticeship and a further two-year improvership before full competence is achieved.

Spale basket-making in Worcestershire

In the Wyre Forest of Worcestershire and in the Furness district of Lancashire, coppice-grown oak provides the raw material for a once important industry; that of *spale* or *spelk* basket-making. Until recently the craft was also practised in Yorkshire, Derbyshire and Shropshire. These oval or round baskets are made of interwoven oak laths or spelks and are still widely used in the Midlands and the North for carrying a great variety of products ranging from shellfish to coke and from animal fodder to cotton waste. In addition to its durability and toughness, the advantage of the spale over osier baskets is the closeness of its weave; indeed so close is the weave that it is possible to carry powdery material in the spale basket. In the past *side slops* or *kidney lips* made in the same manner as spale baskets were widely used for seed sowing.

Processes

The spale basket is almost bowl-shaped and usually measures 2 ft to 3 ft across the rim. The rim, known as the *bool*, is made of hazel, though ash or even oak may be used as an alternative. The process of making the basket begins with the shaping of the bool. Coppice-grown hazel rods are softened by boiling or steaming until quite pliable. Each rod is then bent to an oval shape and the two loose ends fastened with a nail.

The oak used for the spelks is coppice-grown, that is the craftsman uses the straight rods growing round the butt or stool of an already felled tree. The oak, which is usually twenty-five or thirty years old with a diameter of some 6 inches must be straight grained and free of knots. Having cut the poles into 4 ft or 6 ft lengths, the bark, which is in great demand in the tanning industry, is removed and the poles are immersed in boiling water and boiled for many hours, until they are quite soft.

Each pole is then quartered by means of a beetle and wedge, and with a fore or billhook each quarter is split into thin strips 1 inch to 3 inches wide and no more than 1/16th inch thick. This process demands great skill, for the spelks have to be of the same width and thickness throughout their length.

Before weaving the spelks have to be trimmed and smoothed with a fine spokeshave, for the nature of the finished basket will be such that this cannot be done after the completion of the whole process. The spelks are next immersed in water and the stouter ribbons are fixed to the bool to form the warp of the basket. The longest of the wide 3-inch spelks is fitted across the centre and successively shorter ones are added until the warp is complete. The thinner ribbons or *chissies* are then interwoven through the warp and around the bool until the whole basket is completed. The strength of the spale basket is due to the fact that moistened pliant oak can be pressed to a new shape and, as the water in the spelks evaporates, they are set to that new shape.

Tools and equipment

Like osier basket-making, the craft of the spale basket-maker depends on skill and dexterity rather than on any elaborate equipment. The tools they require are few and simple.

Boiler. The boiler used for boiling spelks is similar to that used by Somerset osier-growers for buffing willow. It consists of a metal tank some 5 ft long, 3 ft wide and 2 ft deep. A fire of shavings is lit in the hearth, the smoke being carried away through to the chimney at the far end of the tank.

Froe. The froe, fromard, doll axe, dill axe, or cleaving axe is an L-shaped tool used by many woodland-workers. That used by the spale basket-maker is small, with a blade of mild steel 6 inches long and a handle at right angles to it some 16 inches long. The blade is sharpened on one side only.

Billhook. Some craftsmen use a billhook instead of a froe for spelk-making. This is a small type of billhook known as a *spar hook* with a sharp pointed blade 7 inches long. Both billhook and froe are inserted in the quartered pole, worked from side to side, so that a thin strip of oak can be ripped off by hand.

1 Boiling the oak for spale basket making, Bewdley, Worcestershire

2 Bewdley spale maker with a finished basket

3 Peeling osiers for baskets, Bideford-on-Avon

4 Making a basket rim at Burrowbridge, Somerset

Beetle and wedge. The wooden beetle used by the craftsman for quartering is usually a home-made affair with a head of apple, pear or elm, with an ash handle. The wedge is usually an L-shaped froe with a blade up to 10 inches wide and a handle of 20 inches. The cleft must pass through the pith of the oak pole to produce symmetrical sections. The froe is levered up and down until the pole is completely split.

Shaving-horse. This is a low bench on which the craftsman sits astride, pressing with his foot so as to hold fast the spelk under the projecting clamp-block. The spelk being thin and springy, is placed on a curved platform on top of the horse.

Another type of brake used for shaving consists of a Y-shaped piece of wood firmly embedded in the ground. Two pieces of wood are passed through the projections of the Y and between them a piece of wood or platform 3 inches in diameter runs at an angle of 45 degrees to the ground. At the end of this platform is a heavy weight which holds the jaws open. A spelk is shaved by placing it along the platform and the jaws are closed by resting the left leg on the lower part of the platform. The spales are shaved with an ordinary spokeshave.

Trug basket-making in Sussex

While in the Midlands and the North the closely woven spale basket is popular, its southern equivalent is the trug. The craft is concentrated in Sussex, particularly in the village of Hurstmonceaux where Thomas Smith began to make trugs in the late eighteenth century. Like spale basket-making, trug-making is a craft that demands great exactitude and skill of a high order, but unlike the craftsmen of the Wyre Forest and Furness, those of Sussex have adopted some mechanical techniques. In the trug-making industry, there is no division of labour, for one man makes a trug from first to last. The result is that each trug bears the unmistakable stamp of a particular craftsman and it is said that the expert will recognise the maker of a trug by the workmanship and finish of the basket.

Processes

Trug-making begins with the shaping of the frame. Ash or chestnut rods are first of all cut into convenient lengths and cleft in two with a froe. The bark is left on the outer surface, while the inner surface is shaved and smoothed with a draw-knife and spokeshave; each rod being clamped in the jaws of a shaving-horse for this purpose. Each rod is reduced to a width of 2 inches and a thickness of $\frac{3}{4}$ inch. The rods are then steamed in an elm steaming chest and when fully pliant each one is placed in a simple oval frame called a setting brake. The overlapping ends of the frame rods are next nailed together. A smaller oval, which will form the handle of the basket is next nailed at right angles to the frame.

For the body of the trug, pollard willow some seven years old is used. A willow pole is cleft repeatedly with beetle and froe to form strips of wood no more than $\frac{1}{8}$ inch thick. In some workshops a finely toothed band-saw is used for cleaving. The boards are next clamped in the shaving-horse and smoothed with draw-knives and spoke-shaves to a crescent shape.

The boards are sorted according to size and curve; the longer, thinner ones with straight ends will be centre boards; shorter ones with slightly tapered ends will be seconds and others with a more pronounced end-taper will be side boards. A medium-sized garden trug will usually have one centre board, which is fitted first; two seconds on each side of it, followed by one pair of side boards. This makes a total of seven boards. Like the frame and handles, boards are steamed and their boatlike shape is obtained by levering each board between two wooden bars.

The various parts of the trug are next assembled. Dried boards are dipped in cold water to make them pliable enough for bending and nailing. The centre board goes in first, followed by the seconds and side boards; each one being nailed to the frame with a pair of nails at each extremity, and a pair in the centre. The nails are beaten in with a flat-headed hammer and clinched. All the boards in a trug overlap in a manner not dissimilar to a clinker-built boat. Cross-pieces of willow are finally added to give the basket stability.

Tools

The tools and equipment of a trug maker are not dissimilar to those of the spale basket-maker. The shaving-horse, the beetle and froe and the spokeshave are of the same type.

Steaming chest. This consists of an elm box some 6 feet long, 2 feet wide and 2 feet deep. A pipe from a boiler nearby leads to it, carrying the steam which will make the hazel or willow pliant.

Draw-knife. This is a two-handled knife some 15 inches long, used for shaping wood while it is clamped in the jaws of a shaving-horse.

Setting-brake. The trug-maker has a large number of these brakes in his workshop. They vary from as little as 8 inches in length to as much as 4 feet. A brake consists of a wooden frame, oval in shape, with blocks of wood at each extremity. A trug frame is shaped on the frames, for as the pliable, steamed hazel dries out, the timber is set to the shape of the frame.

Other ordinary carpenter's tools required by the trug-maker are a saw, usually a bow-saw for cutting out, a flat-headed hammer and a pair of pincers.

CHAPTER TWO

Ropes and Nets

The principal raw materials of the rope and net making industries are 'bast' fibres, which are the cellulose cells which support the stem of tall upright plants. Hemp, one of the principal fibres used, may grow from 10 to 15 feet in height, and although in the past, appreciable quantities of hemp were grown in some parts of Britain, especially Dorset, today all the requirements of the industry are imported. Marine ropes are chiefly manufactured from Manila hemp (*musatextilis*). This is obtained from the conjoint leaf stalk, which forms the stem of the non-edible plantain. The fibre is obtained by cutting the tree down near the root and stripping off the leaves. The various layers produce varying types of fibre; those towards the centre of the stem being white in colour and fine in texture, whilst the outside coverings are dull brown and coarse. Sisal, which is obtained from the fleshy leaves of one of the many varieties of agave, is also widely used for rope-making. This, which comes mainly from East Africa, is a clear white fabric and is mainly used for making binder and baler twine and packing cords and twines. New Zealand hemp, which has a brownish colour and is softer than Manila, is less important than it was, while St Helena hemp and the white Mauritius hemp are also used in small quantities. In recent years synthetic fibres have become increasingly important in the industry.

The practice of matting rope by plaiting or of twisting fibre, strips of hide and hair, goes back almost to the dawn of man's existence on earth, for even in Palaeolithic times, some form of cordage was necessary, for the fishing activities of riverside and coastal dwellers. A cave painting from eastern Spain, said to date from Palaeolithic or Mesolithic times, shows a man climbing down a cliff face using a rope. In the ancient Near East too, ropes were widely used and the pyramids and other monuments constructed by vast gangs of workers must have required great quantities of strong rope

14

in their building; indeed in all early constructional work, ropes were essential pieces of equipment, being the only means by which large gangs of men could apply their combined strength to build the huge monuments of antiquity. 'From as early as 4000 B.C. there is evidence of reed rope in Egypt, while examples of rope made from flax, the fibre of the date palm, grass, halfa, papyrus and camel hair have been found. In addition, the various stages in the manufacture of rope are depicted in ancient monuments; the spinning, twisting the strands and laying the rope.'[1] The ships of Syracuse, which sailed the Mediterranean in 200 B.C., were rigged with ropes made of hemp grown in the Rhone Valley.[2]

In Britain too, the craft of rope-making is of great antiquity, and in the city of London alone, it is said to have been carried out continuously from Roman times. In the Middle Ages the Corders of the Ropery were among the earliest of the craftsmen to be established as a guild, although that guild was merged with the Grocers' Company in the mid-fourteenth century. The growing strength of Britain as a maritime power, led to the rapid development of the rope-making industry, and ropeyards were established in most coastal towns and villages.

Rope-making in Dorset
Bridport in Dorset attained pre-eminence as the centre of the rope-making industry, and soon became known as the main producer in Britain of 'twine, string, pack thread, netting, cordage and ropes . . . and the sails for shipping of every kind as well as sacking for hammocks and all kinds of bag and tarpaulin'.[3] As early as the thirteenth century, Bridport was granted a charter to supply the British Navy with cordage. King John, who visited Bridport in 1201 and 1204 'must have been impressed by the growing industry, for in 1211 he sent orders to Bridport for cloth for ships' cables. Two years later he wrote again commanding that "night and day as many ropes for ships both large and small and as many cables as you can and twisted yarn for cordage for ballistae" were to be made with all speed'.[4]

The Middle Ages saw a steady growth in the Bridport rope-making industry and by 1388 it had become sufficiently established for six ropers to leave the town to establish a rope-making industry on the Tyne. It is significant that a northern Guild of Ropers had a Coat of Arms similar to that of Bridport and carried the same motto 'May hemp bind them that honour won't'. Undoubtedly one of the main reasons why Bridport became pre-eminent in the manufacture of cordage was that the soil and climate of Dorset were particularly suitable for the growth of hemp and flax and the early industry was stimulated by the demands of fishermen and boat builders, who flourished on the Dorset coast. Despite restrictive practices, which forced many Bridport rope makers to migrate to the freer atmosphere of the north of England, Bridport 'with its superlative hemp and flax and with its long start over other centres of production',[5] had achieved by the end of the sixteenth century, a virtual monopoly of rope production in England.

There was nevertheless a decline in the industry in the early eighteenth century as a result of competition from naval ropeyards at Woolwich, Deptford, Portsmouth and Plymouth, as well as the silting up of Bridport harbour, until the second half of the century saw the return of prosperity to the industry. But whereas in the past, the main product of Bridport was cordage, in the late eighteenth century nets became the most important product. Rope walks still survived and the craft was carried out by a large number of independent rope makers who operated in ropeyards, often in elongated gardens at the back of their homes. St Michael's Lane in the town, for example, had at one time as many as forty-one rope walks and the large number of alleyways running back from the main streets of the town were all used for rope-making. These alleyways gave Bridport its characteristic shape, which has survived to this day.

At the turn of the nineteenth century, a contemporary writer noted that 'the manufacture of Bridport perhaps flourishes more than at any other former time and furnishes employment not only for the inhabitants of the town, but for those likewise of the neighbouring villages to the extent of ten miles in circumference. It consists of seines and nets of all sorts, lines, twines and similar cordage and sail cloth.'[6] The industry was very much a family industry, with men, women and children being occupied. Women were paid at a rate of eight pence a day for spinning hemp and making nets, while children employed on turning a wheel in the rope walk were paid two or three pence per day.

As in the wool textile trade in Yorkshire, Wales and elsewhere, hemp merchants who organised the manufacturing processes were common in the Bridport district. Samuel Gundry, for example, was a merchant and possibly a banker, who as early as 1665 purchased the hemp crop, issued it to families for conversion into yarn and nets in their homes, and then marketed the goods. Until well on into the nineteenth century, most of the net-making was carried on as out-work in the cottages of Bridport and the surrounding countryside and methods of braiding by hand were handed down the generations from mother to daughter. Net-making was organised from a central factory; twine was delivered weekly and the finished nets were col-lected when next week's work was delivered. John Claridge esti-mated that in 1793 there were 1800 rope and net makers in Bridport and a further 7000 people employed in the trade in the surrounding countryside. The money earned by women outworkers supplemented agricultural wages earned by the menfolk. This helped to give the Dorset rural working class a comparatively high standard of living. Thus in 1821 with the farm worker earning from 8 shillings to 10 shillings and his wife adding 5 shillings a week, it was claimed that the country labourer was better off than his town counterpart.

During the nineteenth century, the amount of locally grown hemp used in the Dorset rope and net industry declined rapidly and by 1893 only 36 acres in the county were devoted to the growing of hemp and flax; most of the raw material required by the industry coming from Russia. The century too witnessed the growth of a factory system in the Bridport industry, with new machines being introduced. By 1820 spinning machines that had to be driven by water were in general use; in 1840 looms for sail cloth were available while in the 1860s hackling machines for the initial processing of hemp and the jumping looms for net-making were introduced. In 1904 the braiding machine was introduced, so that only small or curved nets were hand made by cottagers in their homes.

Rope- and net-making is still the staple industry of Bridport but, as the result of amalgamation and rationalisation, the industry is in the hands of one large industrial complex—Bridport-Gundry Limited. In 1900 there were fifteen large and independent factories in existence. The processes of twine and net-making are now highly mechanised in modern efficient factory buildings, but oddly enough outwork still persists. In 1961 Gundry's had three vans which went out weekly to collect and deliver in the villages, and had more people on its books as outworkers than as factory workers. Small nets such as billiard nets and some curved fishing nets are still made by village women. Today there is no ropeyard at Bridport, the last at Bourton, which employed twelve people being closed early in the present century, and Bridport today is the centre of a flourishing net-making industry, whose products are sold throughout the world.

Inland rope-making

In addition to the rope and net making industry in West Dorset and in hundreds of other coastal towns and villages, inland roperies were equally important and many rural villages and country towns had their rope makers, who were mainly concerned with making ropes, nets, twine and halters for an agricultural market.

Although the country rope-maker has virtually disappeared, a rope walk established in 1841 was until recently producing hand-made cordage for the farming population of St Ives in Huntingdon-shire. A rope walk at Lancaster, established in 1628 and another at Dursley in Gloucestershire established in 1600 were in production in the 1930s, while the celebrated craftsman, who spins rope in Peak Cavern, Derbyshire, still works on a part-time basis. Since the sixteenth century, rope has been made in the limestone areas of the Castleton district, in conditions of considerable discomfort, according to Herbert Marrison, the last of the ropers 'working in the mouth of a cavern which hangs with icicles in winter and runs with water in summer'. Nevertheless shelter from the wind and shade from the sun were important considerations in the location of rope works, for in many places trees were planted along the sides of rope walks to provide shelter. Often these long avenues of trees provide the key to the location of old rope walks, while in some districts long narrow gardens attached to cottages may denote the location of an old ropery.

Until the 1930s, many rural rope walks still persisted. In the West of England they were to be found at Dorchester, Yeovil, Melksham, Ilminster and Bridgwater, while in south-east England there were flourishing rope walks at Hailsham, Maidstone and Lewes. Accord-ing to the survey of rural industries carried out in the 1920s, the following rope walks were in full production in rural England at the time:[7] Dorchester, Yeovil, Melksham, Ilminster, Hailsham, Maid-stone, Lewes, Dursley,[8] Moreton-in-the-Marsh, Chipping Norton, Witney and Banbury, Retford (two walks), Newark, Worksop, Mansfield, Tuxford, Gainsborough, Lincoln, Wragby, Matlock, Castleton, Cambridge, Peterborough, Hitchin, Shelford, St Ives,

Raunds, Stoke Bruern, Woburn Sands, Boxmoor, Bedale, Hawes, Barnard Castle, Melton, Thornton Dale, Kirkby Moorscot (two walks), Pocklington (two walks), Driffield, Kilham, Bridlington, Hunmanby, Otley, Ripon, Chester le Street, Berwick on Tweed (three walks), Kendal, Penrith, Lancaster, Norwich, Chelmsford and Haverhill. In addition to these strictly rural rope walks, concerned mainly with supplying cordage for the farming population, there were a number of rope walks concerned with supplying fishermen's twine and net at such places as Lowestoft, Yarmouth and King's Lynn. At Lowestoft and Yarmouth net twine was sent out to out-workers, who made nets in their homes for the fishermen of the two towns.

In general, the rural roperies in agricultural areas such as East Anglia and the East Riding of Yorkshire persisted longer and were more numerous than coastal roperies concerned with providing ropes for the maritime trade. The old technique of spinning on walks also persisted longer, for by the beginning of the present century machinemade ropes were being produced in great quantities by the rope-makers of Bridport, Gateshead and other coastal towns. In general rope-making in these coastal towns was usually in the hands of large-scale organisations and was not carried out by small, indivi-dual family firms. Nevertheless a few large rope walks did persist in some coastal towns until recently. At Cardiff, for example, a rope walk over half a mile long was in use until 1964 and the rope maker was concerned with making both hand spun and machine spun ropes for the maritime trade.

Over a long period various descriptions have been applied to different constructions of ropes. The principal ones are:

Cordage. General description used for all forms of rope, cord, lines and twines.

Rope. The composition of more than six threads, formed into three or more strands. The threads or yarns are twisted together to form a strand, and three or more of the strands are laid together to form a rope.

Twine. One or more yarns twisted together, made from soft hemp, jute, manila or sisal. Of these, sisal is usually used for packing pur-poses and binder or harvester twine, while manila is used for making nets for the fishing industry.

Hawser laid. Three strands, each consisting of a number of yarns, twisted together to form a rope.

Shroud laid. Four strands, each consisting of a number of yarns twisted together to form a rope, which is mainly used for running gear and over pulleys, as the surface wear is more evenly distributed.

Cable or water laid. Three complete ropes laid together again form a cable laid rope. This is used when elasticity is required as for towing ropes.

Processes

The first process in making a rope is to clean the fibres, ensuring that they are parallel, straight and free of impurities. This sorting process is known as hackling, and it is a task usually performed by women, even when modern machines are used for the process. Until recently in the smaller rope yards hackling boards were widely used for the initial treatment of hemp fibres. The hackle board is a wooden block some 16 inches long and 5 inches wide, studded with strong, tapered steel pins about 5 inches long. To ensure that the fibre is thoroughly hackled, the rope-maker has a series of these boards, with prongs diminishing in size and set more closely together. The hackler takes a handful or 'streak' of hemp, wrapping one end firmly around his hand and distributing a little whale or linseed oil over it. 'Care and particular attention must be paid', said a nineteenth-century encyclopaedist, 'that they do not use too great a quantity of oil, as in such case it will prevent the yarn from imbibing its proper proportion of tar, and thereby prove a serious injury'.[9] Usually a pint of oil per hundredweight of hemp is enough to facilitate the hackling process. The hemp is struck against the pins and drawn through repeatedly until all the fibres are parallel. First the top half of the streak is hackled, then the bottom half. The streak is then weighed, doubled up to prevent tangling, and laid aside ready for spinning.

The hackling machine has two sets of chains fitted with steel hackle pins, the first chain carrying the first to the second which travels at a greater speed, thereby combing and cleaning it. The first is fed to the machine in separate streaks and leaves it in a continuous ribbon or sliver. The process is repeated several times and the fibre then reaches the second process, called drawing. Here again the combing process is continued and the fibre emerges from the machine in fine slivers, which are controlled by the variations in the speed of the feed and delivery, according to the size of the yarn required.

Spinning in most rope works today is carried out over automatic or gile spinners, the first spinning machine being invented in 1799 by a Mr Chapman. The spinning process involves the conversion of the sliver, with its parallel fibres into yarn. Traditionally, spinning is performed by hand. The spinner is laden round the waist with the hackled hemp, with the ends at the back. From the middle of the streak, he draws out some fibres, twisting them between finger and thumb, and attaches them to one of the four hooks on the large spinning wheel. This wheel, some 3 feet in diameter, to which the whirls are attached, is turned by a crank handle, a job usually done by a young boy. 'The spinning wheel', said Abraham Rees 'must be kept turning a constant regular pace, otherwise the yarn so spun will lose its principal support, which is its proper turn or twist, and will be little stronger than a parcel of straight hemp laid together, which would break in warping or straining up.' Slowly the spinner walks backwards along the rope walk, drawing out more fibres as he does so. He ensures that the fibres emerge equally from both sides of the bundle and with his left hand he makes sure that the yarn is smooth surfaced. As he walks back, the spinner throws the yarn over T-shaped stakes embedded in the ground at regular intervals along the rope walk. When thread of sufficient length has been spun, and in early nineteenth-century ropeyards the length was supposed to be 160 fathoms for a quarter of a day's work, the boy at the wheel detaches the end from the twisting hooks and fixes the end to a winding reel. Slowly the spinner walks forward along the rope walk, holding the end of the yarn to prevent it unravelling and keeping it taut throughout the journey. The process is repeated until the reel is full with about 250 pounds of well-spun yarn. Spinning is one of the most skilled of all processes in a rope yard and a good spinner may well walk many miles in a day's work. Rees tells us that in 1819 a spinner was paid seven pence per quarter day for his work, while hacklers, wheel turners and wheel tenders (responsible for splicing threads and winding spun yarn) were paid six pence per quarter day for their work.

After spinning, the yarn is made into strands, either in the rope walk or in the rope-making shop. In the latter, the so-called house machines are used and this is the method adopted in most modern

Fig. 2 Hand ropemaker spinning yarn. A streak of hackled hemp hangs
from his waist and is spun by the boy on the wheel

roperies. The yarn is put on bobbin banks or racks, drawn off and formed into strands on a machine a few feet away. This is known as 'a Former', the strands being wound on a bobbin. When a length of strands has been formed, the bobbins are put into a closing machine, which is then set in motion to close the strands into a finished rope.

The rope walk is usually a long building furnished with rail tracks. The spun yarn is put on bobbin racks or banks, and when drawn off is passed through a metal register plate, pierced with a series of holes, which are formed in circles corresponding to the outer and inner yarns of the strand of rope. After the yarns have been passed through this plate, they are drawn through a tube in a fixed or standing part of the rope making machine, known as 'a fore-board'. The strand is drawn through the tube and attached to the sledge or traveller, which is a machine furnished with a series of four revolving hooks. This machine travels down the rope walk on the rail track, hauling out the strands, at the same time imparting the twist required. When the predetermined length of strand has been drawn off, it is cut from the tube and attached to hooks on the for-thoard, similar to those on the traveller. When sufficient twist has been imparted into the strand, the strands on the traveller are taken off their respective hooks and fixed to a centre hook ready for laying together. Between the foreboard and the traveller is a machine known as 'a top cart' on which is fixed a tapered cone of hardwood with three or four grooves in it. The strands are placed in their res-pective grooves and the hooks on the foreboard are caused to revolve. This operation causes the top cart to travel in the direction of the foreboard, and results in the strands twisting together to form a rope. According to the speed at which the top cart travels, the lay of the strands in the rope becomes longer or shorter as required. The effort of the revolving hooks is assisted by men stationed along the rope, each armed with a three-foot long stick called 'a woolder'. These are levers to twist the rope in the required direction.

In most cases, before ropes are laid spun yarn is tarred by drawing it through boiling tar. 'Tarring the yarn', says Rees, 'is a process which should be particularly attended to, being extremely careful that the tar is not boiling too fast nor too slow: if too fast the tar will not stay in the yarn; it not hot enough the tar will not sufficiently penetrate the yarn.' In many disused rope yards, the remains of a tarring shop may be seen. A horsedriven capstan for winding tarred yarn was a common piece of equipment, and it was essential that the capstan turned slowly and steadily to wind the rope that was passed through the boiler of heated tar. If, for some reason, the capstan stopped, it was considered necessary to remove the rope from the boiler without delay. Three men were needed for this task—one to heat the tar, one to pay the yarn into the boiler and another to wind it on to the capstan.

Undoubtedly the methods of rope making that have persisted in rope yards to the present day have continued almost unchanged from prehistoric times. The most laborious process of all is perhaps the laying of cables, consisting of those complete ropes laid together to provide a strong, elastic cable. In the past this required the strength of as many as eighty men and the use of a large heavy top to produce a cable that could be as much as 24 inches in diameter.

CHAPTER THREE

Straw Plait and Rush Mats

The technique of weaving rush, grass or straw is one that goes back to prehistoric times and there is evidence to suggest that by the fifteenth century the craft of straw-plaiting and hat-making flourished in many parts of Europe. By 1575, for example, the straw hat merchants of Tuscany had been formed into a corporation and that region with Leghorn at its centre later became the world's most important centre of plaiting. In Saxony, too, the tradition of straw hat making goes back to the sixteenth century, while in the Liege district straw hat making is said to date from the middle ages.

Straw plaiting in Bedfordshire

Straw plaiting was introduced into Britain in the sixteenth century by the Lorrainers, and the industry became established in Bedfordshire, Buckinghamshire and Hertfordshire. As time went on and straw hats gained in popularity, plaiting together with lace-making became one of the most important industries of the south-east Midlands and by 1851 eighty per cent of the total workers in the hat trade lived in the region.[1] Straw plaiting dominated home life in Luton, Dunstable and the surrounding villages, plait schools flourished, weekly plait markets drew thousands of people to the market towns of the region and the whole economy and social life of the south-east Midlands was tied up with the straw-plaiting trade. Other specialised craftsmen, such as hat block makers and box makers were entirely dependent on the plaiters and hat makers. Although plaiting was primarily a female occupation, most boys were also taught plaiting 'and attended plaiting schools until they took up farm work at about fourteen or fifteen. Even the men did plaiting as a spare time occupation'.[2]

Until the second decade of the twentieth century the straw hat industry flourished and the plaiters working in their own homes found a ready market for their plait in the dozens of hat factories in the

Fig. 3 Straw hatmakers, *c.* 1827. The lady in the middle is splitting straws by hand while the lady on the left is actually making up a hat

5 Preparing the top at a Cardiff rope walk

6 The top cart in a Cardiff rope walk

7 Products of a ropemaker on sale at Carmarthen market

8 A marram grass worker weaving mats

region. In most cases, however, the plait was first of all sold to mid-dlemen, the straw dealers who travelled from village to village. Plait-makers were also extremely important, and raw material was bought and the finished plait sold at these markets. On Monday, Luton had its market, on Tuesday Hitchin, Wednesday Dunstable Thursday Hemel Hempstead, Friday Tring and Shefford, while on Saturday a market was held at Toddington. For years there were open air markets, and in some towns they continued to be so, for as long as they existed. The plait-makers set up their stalls in the streets, but in the 1860s and 70s, at a period when the plaiting industry was on the wane, Luton, Dunstable and Hitchin had their special plait halls. Here all dealings in straw; the buying of raw material and the selling of finished plait to the middlemen were carried out. The plait was in time sold by the straw dealers to the dozens of hat factories located in the region, or it was sold to the hundreds of 'makers up' who carried out their task in their homes. The latter were mainly concerned with making the cheaper variety of hats. Again, some of the makers-up did work for the large factories and until the 1920s home work was an essential feature of the hat making industry.

Plaiting was, however, a distinct trade and plaiters were not concerned with making finished hats. Unthreshed wheat straw is preferred for plaiting and it was a common practice for the arable farmers of the south-east Midlands to reserve a proportion of their wheat crop for the straw dealers, who visited the various farms of the district selecting and grading the straw, the best type for plaiting being a long clean stem. After cutting off the ears, the straws were tied into bunches by the dealers, each bundle weighing fifty-six pounds or a hundredweight. In some cases, too, before the straw was sold to the plait makers, the stems had to be stripped, that is the leaf had to be removed, flattened stems had to be thrown away and each straw cut to a length of nine or ten inches. They were then placed in a wooden box and bleached with molten sulphur or dyed. Grading into various thicknesses was done with a simple but efficient straw sorter. This consisted of a wooden frame fitted with a series of wire sieves at the top. A bundle of straws was jolted lightly over each sieve, starting with the finest and finishing with the coarsest. The appropriate grade of straw fell through the mesh into a box below. They were then tied into bundles of six inches or so, ready to be sold at the plait markets or directly to the plait-makers.

The plaiter usually made up the straws into plait either in the form of 'whole straw plait', using each straw in the round, or the straw was used in 'split' form to make a much finer variety of plait, as good as the best Italian variety. Although in early days straw splitting was done with an ordinary knife, in the first quarter of the nineteenth century, a simple but effective straw splitter was introduced. This consisted of a small head with blades radiating from the centre. The tool was a small version of the basket-maker's cleaver. The head was attached at rightangles to a handle some 6 inches long, and a straw splitter could be equipped with any number of blades ranging from three to thirteen. In later days more elaborate straw splitters were introduced: for example, a piece of wood pierced by four holes with splitters inside each hole was a common form in the mid-nineteenth century.

Before they were plaited the straws had to be flattened by being passed between the beech or boxwood rollers of a small mangling device known as a 'splint mill'. These mills were screwed to cottage doorposts, and children were often given the boring task of operating them. In some districts, too, an ordinary rolling pin was used for flattening straws and splints.

The plaiter armed with a bundle of whole straws or splints under her left arm worked at great speed, drawing out each straw from the bundle as it was required, moistening it with the lips and plaiting a number simultaneously. The straws in use at the same time were known as 'ends' and they ranged in number from three to seven. A great variation of pattern could be made by varying the weave. The ends of the straws that projected from the plait had to be cut off with the knife and the work had to pass through the rollers of a plait mill. This was similar in shape to the splint mill, but the rollers in this case were grooved to take the various widths of plait.

The plait was then coiled into scores, coils of twenty yards, and sold at the markets. It is said that one source of great loss to the hat manufacturers in the first half of the nineteenth century was the widespread practice of giving short measure. In 1852 the Straw Hat Manufacturers Association was set up to combat this and it continued to operate for over twenty years.

Rush mat making

The county of Anglesey attained considerable fame as the only county in Wales where marram grass growing on sand dunes provided the raw material for an important industry. This peculiarly tough reed, known in Anglesey as *morhesg*, grows profusely on the west coast of the island, particularly in the parishes of Llanddwyn and Newborough. For many centuries, no one knows exactly how many, the inhabitants of Newborough have made a scanty living by plaiting this material 'into mats for the farmer's haystacks, barn roofs and cucumber frames as well as into nets and cordage for the fishermen'.[3]

In the mid-nineteenth century, Newborough was described as 'the most miserable spot in Anglesey' and it was the abject poverty of the village that struck all travellers to the county. Its menfolk worked long hours for a miserably low wage on the limited amount of agricultural land, while the women attempted to eke out those low wages by making mats in their homes.

Undoubtedly, the mat-making industry of Newborough came into existence as an antidote to poverty, in an area not well blessed with natural advantages. Although mat-making was traditionally women's work, in the palmy days of the industry in the mid-nineteenth century, when the demand for Newborough mats was heavy, men, women and children were engaged in the craft, 'and every house was a little factory supplying not only the district around, but even parts of Caernarvonshire, Denbighshire and Flintshire'.[4]

The industry never extended far beyond the village of Newborough and the reason given for this was the fact that the craft of mat-making required 'traditional skill, which is either hereditary or acquired in early childhood'.[5] It was said that a girl coming into the village older than fourteen years of age could never learn to make the mats as quickly or as well as a native.

The reed was cut in the summer months, usually in late August or September and although scythes were occasionally used, the most common tool for harvesting was a broadbladed reaping hook. The best raw material was two-year-old reed, for the growth of the first year was considered too weak and that of the third year contained too many withered stalks (*morhesg llwyd*) to be of use to the mat-maker. One writer in the 1920s noted that 'the cutting of grass has been carried on for so long by each family, that now every woman goes to her own particular area of the sand dune and claims it as her own property, from which no one else is allowed to cut any sea reed'.[6]

The method of harvesting was as follows:

A bunch of grass was grasped with one hand and cut with a sharp stroke of the hook. A bunch of grass was described as a *fres* or *freesan* and each bunch consisted of four or six stalks growing from a single root or stool. Each stalk with a pointed end measured from 12 to 36 inches in length. The plant was cut as near the stool as possible, usually some 2 inches below the level of the sand. With careful cutting, the stool would continue to bear its crop of usable reed for many years. Since the reed was always cut while green it had to be left in the open air to ripen for some weeks before it could be used.

2. Four or five handfuls of cut stalks were heaped together and in the evenings, before leaving the dunes, the harvesters carried the crop to dry sheltered positions. The reed was spread out to dry and ripen under the mellowing influences of sun and wind until they were hard, dry and white in colour.

3. The reed (*taenfeydd*) was then gathered into bundles, known as *geifr* and stooked, with their roots at the bottom. Again they were left at this stage for some days, or even weeks, depending on the weather.

4. The unusable grey stalks were then shaken out and two bundles of reed placed together; the head of one against the root of the other and bound tightly with a reed rope some four feet long to form an *ysgub forhesg* (reed sheaf).

5. After further ripening and the shaking out of all grey stalks, the bundles were again bound, but this time with the roots all facing the same way. The sheaves were then placed in water to soften before they could be used.

Harvesting usually took at least a month, depending on the weather, and the crop was then brought into the house. Each woman provided herself with enough material for her own use, but some of the older women who were unable to gather their own raw material bought reed from their neighbours. In the nineteenth century they could buy reed 'in bundles from Aberffraw paying about one shilling for each bundle'.[7] At that time 'the younger girls form into groups of half a dozen and go to work together in some empty house, thus keeping their homes tidy. As most of the houses have only one living room, home work is very inconvenient when the house is occupied by a large family, and by meeting together, the work is less tedious for the young girls. The wives are not able to leave the house and they prefer to work at home'.

Williamson, a local historian, described the method of working as follows in 1903:

Two or three groups of stalks are inserted into the edge away from the plaiter. As a stalk is inserted it is plaited with the three on the right, using the right hand to plait and the left to hold the work. It is then grasped with the right hand and plaited with the left until the plaited stalk takes the place of that plaited with the right hand. It is obvious that the number of stalks have to be an odd number, and the thumn of the left hand is always used to turn the plait upwards. The number of straws in a plait is eleven, but in order to make the edges rigid, thirteen stalks are used. . . . The mat must consist of lengths of eight plaits, every plait to be eight Welsh yards, each yard being forty inches. After sewing strips of plait to strips of plait—rought side to rough side and smooth to smooth—to make a length of matting eight yards long, the mat is folded and the two sides again joined. The folded mat is opened so that each is sixteen plaits wide and four yards long. A narrow plait of five straws, to sew the edges, is made to prevent unravelling. After folding, the mat is sold to merchants, who keep it dry and safe for the next hay harvest, when they are taken to the markets for sale to farmers.[8]

The method of plaiting in the 1920s was considerably simpler than that described by Owen Williamson.

The grass is two or three feet long. To plait it, six or seven straws of the same size are taken and by knocking the bunch against the knee the worker gets them in order for the plaiting. There are about six of these bunches in each plait and the width of the plait is about four inches. All the plaiting is done by the right hand; the left putting in the new bunches when the old strand is becoming thin, and keeping the plait in position. This method keeps the right edge always smooth, whereas the left edge where the new bunches are joined in, is rough. A leather strap fastened to the ceiling forms a loop to support the plait. When long enough the plaited end is weighted down by a poker or some such object, or kept in position by the foot. In plaiting, the worker is seated and has the work about level with her face.[9]

The Newborough rush mat making industry persisted until recent times, but the advent of corrugated iron sheets for storing hay on farms decreased the demand for thatching mats, which was the main product of the industry. Thatching mats were used for throwing over haystacks until the farmer found time to thatch them, and it is said that these mats kept the hay in better condition than corrugated roofs, since they allowed the sweat to evaporate into the air. Thatching mats measured some three yards long by one yard wide. To make them the plaiter made a four inch plait some eighty yards long. With a sacking needle and thread of plaited grass, the plait was joined together until it formed nine lengths sewn edge to edge.

In addition to mats the Newborough craftsmen produced considerable quantities of grass rope (known locally as *tannau*) which was widely used for packing glassware, pottery and polished furniture as well as for packing barbed wire for transportation.

Early in the present century, the Newborough Mat Makers Association was founded, and a successful attempt was made to search for new markets for the products of Newborough. Horticultural mats, particularly strawberry mats, were made in considerable quantities, as were table mats, floor mats, foot stools and baskets. By the end of the first world war, the mat makers of Newborough were no longer dependent on only two products—thatching mats and grass ropes. The Association too improved cooperation between the craftsmen and had its depot in the village for storing mats. In the 1920s members of the Association were paid three shillings for each mat they delivered at the depot; a great change from the conditions in the late nineteenth century when:

There was no co-operation among the makers and all trade was done by barter. Each worker made her purchases at the grocer's or butcher's shop, giving the shopkeeper so many mats in payment. These the shopkeeper stored until local merchants came round in early summer to buy them. The merchants took the mats to the fairs held in July at Cricieth and Pwllheli, and here the farmers would buy their annual stock of mats. As a rule, the worker was given food to the value of 1s. 10d. for each mat and the shopkeeper sold them for about 3s. Thus the shopkeeper made a profit both on the mats and on the food given in exchange to the mat maker.[10]

Nevertheless, despite the formation of the Mat Makers Association, the last thirty years has witnessed the complete disappearance of this once important industry.

Closely related to the craft of mat-making was that of making besoms or brooms near the villages of Rhosneigr, Valley and Aberffraw. This was a part-time craft carried out by farm labourers and others who lived near the sand dunes. All the craftsman required was a number of broom sticks and strong cord for fastening the reeds. The besoms were made by tying a bunch of reeds, some three feet long along the middle, fitting the handle in the middle and tying the tuft of reed firmly to it. In the 1920s these, which were greatly favoured for such tasks as whitewashing, were sold for threepence each.

CHAPTER FOUR

Paper

Paper-making has been widely practised in Britain for nearly 500 years. The first record is of Tate's mill near Stevenage in Hertfordshire in 1490, but it seems that this ceased to operate within a few years. The industry occurs widely in relatively popular parts of the country, but was in the past found also in the most unexpected rural locations. In Wales, for example, many paper mills were found at Whitebrook, a rural valley in Monmouthshire, while in the late eighteenth and early nineteenth centuries the industry flourished in a remote valley near Crickhowell in Brecknockshire. Undoubtedly paper-making came to these remote valleys because there was a plentiful and never-failing supply of pure soft water, used not only for driving mill machinery, but also for the actual process of manufacturing paper.

A factory system seems to have entered the paper-making industry comparatively early: 'When John Spilman erected a mill for making paper on the back of the River Darent at Dartford in Kent in 1586, he introduced what may be regarded as the earliest factory conditions in England.[1] In this factory there was division of labour and a certain amount of mechanisation. The manufacturing process in sixteenth-century Kent differed but little from the techniques practised in ancient China and Egypt, and while 'each succeeding century has witnessed modifications in Spilman's technique . . . these constituted improvements of existing methods rather than fundamental changes'. Early paper making was often combined with corn grinding; both operations being carried out in the same building.

Until approximately 1860, the paper mills of Britain, especially in the rural parts, depended heavily on adequate supplies of rags, which were collected from all over a region. The sorting of rags was undertaken by women and children, and Abraham Rees in his *Cyclopaedia* of 1819[2] described how they were 'seated on benches, in a large room

full of old linen, before a chest or box which is divided into six cases
to receive as many different sorts of rags. Each woman has a piece of
pasteboard, hung from her girdle and extended on her knees, upon
which, with a long, sharp knife, she unrips seams and stitches, and
scrapes off all filth.' The quality and composition of rags affected the
quality of finished paper, the best being made from white linen rags
with a small proportion of cotton included. Occasionally such substances as nettle stalks, straw, hay, spent hops and thistle down were
added to rags for special types of paper.

Sometimes the rags, after sorting, were soaked in water, pressed
into balls and placed in a damp cellar to ferment for two months or
more.

During this process they became straw-coloured, but lost nearly
one quarter of their weight, and became fragile facilitating the subsequent process of macerating and cleaning. The evil-smelling rags
were cut into fragments with chopping knives hinged to wooden
blocks and worked up and down by hand. They were then washed in
running water and rubbed by hand in an effort to remove the yellow
tinge, the presence of which was responsible for the pleasant creamy
tinge of old paper.

From the early nineteenth century bleaching with chemicals was
usual in paper mills.

Rag-cutting was considered unhealthy work, for not only were the
rags dusty, but they could also carry infectious diseases. A female
ragger—and sorting was traditionally a girl's work—was paid an
average wage of half-a-crown to three shillings a week in 1843.
Usually they worked a twelve-hour day, six days a week, with an hour
for dinner and a few minutes for breakfast. Some sorters worked at
night, and no holidays at all were allowed. Rag-cutters were paid
three shillings and six pence to four shillings a week, and both boys
and girls were engaged in this task.

The next process was the pulping of rags under the pounding of
battery hammers. Diderot describes how the rags were thrown into a
solid oak or stone trough, lined with lead and subjected to pounding
for three days.[3] Each battery of stamping machines consisted of from
three to eight heavy hammers, somewhat similar to those in a fulling
mill. The stamps used for the first beating were tipped with spikes
to tear the rags apart, and the troughs in which they pounded were
fed constantly by a stream of running water, which washed away

impurities. Woven horsehair mats prevented the escape of the pulp. 'On the following day, the rags were transferred to a second set of water troughs and beaten with a lightly shod set of stamps. Half a ton of water was needed to prepare sufficient fibre for one pound of paper.' Lastly the pulp was pounded by all-wooden stamps in a tank of static water. No running water at all was used during the third stamping, for fear of washing the pulp itself away. The Goldengrove and Glangrwyne mills in Brecknockshire, for example, each had one set of beating engines in 1851, but it seems likely that in both mills there were true beating engines or hollanders rather than the older, more primitive stamping machines. The beating engine dating from about 1770 is basically the type of machine used in a modern paper mill. It consisted of a solid wooden roll fitted with thirty-six metal knives revolving in a covered tub over ten other metal bars or on a stone bed plate in a revolving drum macerating the rags. A constant stream of water flowed into the engine and the rags were completely mixed and cut up into a smooth pulp. For printing paper, size, usually consisting of a mixture of powdered alum and oil, was added at the beating stage so as to provide a smooth surface in the finished paper. The engine boy or engineer was paid an average wage of two shillings a week in 1843.

One of the most important craftsmen in a paper mill was the vat-man, responsible for the actual moulding of paper. This task was carried out in a lofty room, well ventilated and with a smooth and even ceiling so that the steam arising from the several vats of pulp did not condense on it and fall in drops, for a single drop falling upon a sheet of paper whilst it is moulding, will beat a hole through it or at least spoil it.

The pulp vats, according to Rees, were coopered vessels, 5 feet in diameter and 2 foot 6 inches deep, but square, stone vats, 6 feet square could also be used. The vat and its contents had to be kept warm, 'by means of a grate introduced at a hole in the side and surrounded on the inside of the vat with a case of copper'. Charcoal was often used for fuelling the fire. Later, steam pipes were installed in vats. The contents of the vat had to be agitated constantly, in early days by a pole with a perforated disc at its tip and later by a mechanical paddle called a hog.

The equipment required by a vatman consisted of a mould and deckle. The mould was a square mahogany frame with its top covered

Fig. 4 Vatman operating the mould and deckle

by a fine wire mesh. This rested loosely within another frame called the deckle, and was essential to ensure straight edges to the sheet of paper. Grasping the mould and deckle, the vatman plunged them into the warm, liquid pulp. 'Sleeves pushed back', said Diderot[4] 'he takes a mould, plunges it steeply into the vat, turns it horizontally and lifts, sieving out a layer of pulp and letting water drain back into the vat. With almost the same motion he gives his mould two shakes —from right to left and from front to back. This matted the fibres both ways and gave the sheet equal tension strength.'

The mould containing the pulp was passed along a bench, called 'a bridge' to another craftsman called a coucher, who removed the deckle and turned the mould over on to a piece of woollen felt. Felt and paper were laid in alternate layers to a height of two feet or more, ready for pressing. The paper and felt were then carefully separated and the paper pressed again. After drying, sizing (if sizing had not been completed in the beating engines) and glazing, the paper was ready for cutting into smaller sheets, ready for despatch from the mill. The size was made from shreds and parings from local tanneries, mixed with alum. This method of paper-making was adopted in numerous rural paper mills in many parts of the country and persisted in some districts until at least the last quarter of the nineteenth century. Basically the processes of paper-making remained unchanged, whether the paper was made by hand or by machine. By 1800 there were as many as 416 paper mills in England and Wales, 49 in Scotland and 60 in Ireland.

The development of the Fourdrinier machine at the beginning of the nineteenth century was an important technical innovation, for it was now possible to produce papers in continuous rolls.[5] In 1803 Bryan Donkin, an engineer engaged by two London stationers, the brothers Fourdrinier, erected the first successful paper-making machine. This was based on the ideas of Louis Robert, a Frenchman who had failed to develop them successfully himself. John Dickinson patented his cylinder machine in 1809, and in 1821 T. B. Crompton patented a device for the drying of a continuous sheet of paper by means of steam-heated cylinders. As a result of such innovations, many of the older type of mills disappeared, so that by 1830 one-half of the paper made in Britain was made by machine. There was a marked concentration of the industry in new industrial districts such as King's Langley, as well as developments in older paper-making towns such as Dartford. Increased productivity, the extension of markets, the development of transport and the need to find additional capital for new equipment forced many of the older mills out of business. It was now an advantage to locate paper mills, not on the banks of crystal streams but in the coalfields, near the source of supply of fuel for driving steam equipment.

During the first half of the nineteenth century too, many experiments were being undertaken to find suitable alternatives to rags, and the introduction of esparto grass in 1857 and wood pulp a few years later accelerated the closure of the smaller mills.

Paper-making today is a vast industrial undertaking, but fundamentally the process is the same as that employed hundreds of years ago, and the machines themselves are the same in essential principles as those first introduced at the beginning of the nineteenth century.

CHAPTER FIVE

Pottery

One of the oldest crafts of mankind is that of making pottery. Since the dawn of civilisation, wherever there was suitable clay, men have used it for making decorative as well as utilitarian objects. Throughout the ages, the techniques of pottery-making have not changed in any important detail, and the methods adopted in modern studio potteries today differ but little from those employed in prehistoric days.

Potteries of old standing are always found near beds of local clay, for the difficulty of transporting such heavy and bulky material determined their site. In Wales, for example, the potteries at Ewenni near Bridgend, at Rumney near Cardiff, and at Buckley in Flintshire, came into existence because of the availability of clay. A second prerequisite is fuel to fire the kilns, for although today electrically fired kilns are found in almost every pottery, in the past it was an advantage for the potter to site his workshops within easy reach of coal supply. Nevertheless, coal was less important than the availability of clay. In Devon, for example, the famous Barum ware of Barnstaple was produced in a district far removed from the nearest coal deposits, as were the potteries at Poole in Dorset, at Hailsham in Sussex and Weatheriggs in Cumberland. Although a large number of old-established potteries still exist, the new demand for handmade earthenware has led to the establishment of a large number of studio potteries in many parts of Britain, particularly in centres of the tourist trade. The craft is perhaps more flourishing now than it has ever been and although many craftsmen produce goods of excellent quality and design the market has also been flooded by quantities of inferior material. Nevertheless, the pottery industry has remained 'an intimate and personal industry, and even when its reputation became world-wide, the personal thread never disappeared'.[1]

The methods adopted by potters are simple, for the art of the potter arises in his ability to treat and shape clay rather than on any elaborate piece of equipment and tools. Until the seventeenth century the majority of potters, operating in all parts of the country, were largely dependent on local raw materials and a local market for the distribution of finished products, the quality of which was only as good as the nature of the local clay allowed it to be. For example, among some potteries in the Vale of Glamorgan, the local clay contained limestone, which tended to act as a flux when the pots were fired and the potters were faced with the difficult task of removing some of the fluxing impurities. As Brears says 'if the local clay was poor, the local people had to make do with poor-quality wares; in areas where fuel was scarce, the wares would be expensive; if the winter was hard, no pots could be made, and therefore as the potters could not afford suitable warehousing facilities, none would be on sale'.[2]

One of the main factors contributing to the rapid development of the pottery industry in the seventeenth century was the emergence of a class of pottery merchants, 'pot mongers' or 'crate sellers' who shook the pottery industry from its medieval simplicity. 'Their effect on the contemporary pottery trade was considerable, for their skilful marketing, well organised transport and provision of warehouses allowed pottery to be sold all the year round, and for the first time brought the country's potteries into open competition with one another.'[3] As a result, many of the more inefficient potteries were forced to close down, and only those in favoured locations, near beds of good quality clay and a plentiful supply of coal for firing were in a position to expand. For some potteries that expansion was rapid, as at Burslem in Staffordshire and Ticknall in Derbyshire. By the mid-seventeenth century, Burslem potteries were almost mass producing ware by moulding rather than throwing, and new techniques of decorating were evolved in the town. The Ticknall pottery, near Burton on Trent, was said to be one of the largest potteries in Britain by the end of the seventeenth century, although little is known about the nature of its products.

By the early eighteenth century Staffordshire reigned supreme as the most important pottery centre in Britain. Two brothers of Dutch–German origin, John and David Elers, not only introduced salt-glaze into the industry but also made a considerable contribution to the methods of refining and mixing clays. As a result of their work,

English pottery could compete in quality with imported Chinese wares. 'Always now the working was towards something akin to porcelain, not only in texture but also in colour, and the next step naturally became white stoneware' (that is, pottery fired at a very high temperature which makes it extremely hard and impervious to liquids), 'the Staffordshire salt glaze, which in its class is unsurpassed today'.[4]

Among other technical innovations of the early eighteenth century was that of surface washing clay with a white Devonshire clay and introducing calcined flint into the clay itself so as to give a white body. One of these flint mills at Cheddleton near Leek, has been preserved and is in process of being restored.

In the 1730s porous moulds for casting were adopted by Staffordshire potteries so that it became possible to produce thinner and lighter bodies as well as more complicated shapes than could be produced by throwing or turning on a lathe. It was now possible to produce thousands of pieces, all exact replicas of one another, with the result that vast quantities could be produced with rapidity with a consequent reduction in price. By the mid-eighteenth century therefore, English produced pottery was within the financial reach of millions and the commercialisation of the Potteries was at hand. Canals and roads were built, new products were introduced and north Staffordshire became the most important pottery producing area in the world.

Preparation of clay

Clay for making pottery is dug in the autumn before the winter rains set in, making the clay beds impossibly waterlogged. For some four months the nearly dry clay is left in large heaps so that it experiences the mellowing influence of frost, snow and ice. During the winter months, the masses are broken up and turned constantly, so that the atmosphere can penetrate in every direction. To do this, traditional clay spades are used. These spades, made of willow and shod with metal sheeting, have an advantage over metal spades in that the clay does not stick to the blade to the same extent as it does to metal. They also also much lighter, a very important point when dealing with heavy material, and since the spade is shaped from a single piece of wood there is no danger of it cracking at the joints.

In Staffordshire a great variety of clays was required. Details are

9 Throwing at the Ewenni Pottery, Glamorgan

10 Women sorting linen rags and the method of fermenting them for making paper

given by Dr Robert Plot in his *Natural History of Staffordshire* of 1686:

> Other potters' clays for the more common wares, there are at many other places, particularly at Horsley Heath in the parish of Tipton; in Monway Field above mentioned, where there are two sorts gotten, one of a yellowish colour mixed with white, the other blewish; the former stiff and weighty, the other more friable and light, which, mixt together, work better than when apart. Of these they make divers sorts of vessels at Wednesbury, which they paint with slip, made of a reddish sort of earth gotten at Tipton. But the greatest pottery they have in this county is carried on at Burslem, near Newcastle under Lyme, where for making their several sorts of pots, they have as many different sorts of clay, which they dig round about the towns, all within half a mile's distance, the best being found nearest the coale, and are distinguish't by their colours and uses as followeth:

> 1. Bottle clay, of a bright whitish streaked yellow colour.

> 2. Hard fire clay of a duller whitish colour, and fuller intersperst with a dark yellow, which they use for their black wares, being mixt with the

> 3. Red binding clay, which is a dirty red colour.

> 4. White clay, so called it seems, though of a blewish colour, and used for making yellow colour'd ware, because yellow is the lightest colour they make any ware of.

> All which they call throwing clays, because they are of a closer texture, and will work on the wheel; which none of the three other clays they call slips, will any of them doe, being of looser and more friable natures; these mixed with water they make into a consistence thinner than a syrup, so that being put into a bucket it will run out through a quill, this they call slip, and is the substance wherewith they paint their wares; whereof the

> 1. Sort is called the orange slip, which before it is work't is of a greyish colour mixt with orange balls, and gives the ware [when annealed] an orange colour.

> 2. The white slip, this before it is work't is of a dark blewish colour, yet makes the ware yellow, which being the lightest

colour they make any of, they call it [as they did the clay above] the white slip.

3. The red slip, made of a dirty reddish clay, which gives wares a black colour.

These clay deposits, says Brears,

> were exceptional, however, and most potteries had a choice of only one or two clays. The great string of potteries lying on the coal-measure pot-clay seams in the North of England were fortunate to be able to dig a red throwing clay, a buff fireclay, and a white clay for slip making. Many other potteries, such as those in Northamptonshire, had only one clay to work from, and this was frequently poor and impure in quality.[5]

Before being used for making pottery, clays have to be treated. There are many methods of doing this, the traditional method being to steep the clay in water in a soaking pit, adding sand if necessary. Simeon Shaw in his *History of the Staffordshire Potteries* (1829) gives details of the so-called 'sun pan' that is still used in a number of country potteries:

> The Sun Kiln is formed usually square, 16 to 20 feet in extent each way, and about 18 inches deep, having at one corner a smaller place, deeper, and lined with slabs or flags. The clay, after being brought out of the mine is spread abroad on the adjoining ground, and frequently turned over by the spade during two or three seasons, that it may be well exposed to the action of the atmosphere (called weathering). Into the smaller vat a quantity of clay is thrown, and by a proper tool blunged in the water by agitation, till all the heavier particles and small stones sink to the bottom; the fluid mass is next poured into a sieve, thro' which it runs into the largest vat, or sun kiln, until the whole surface is covered to the depth of three or four inches, which is left to be evaporated by solar action. When this is partly accomplished, another layer, and a third and fourth are added, until the mass is from 12 to 18 inches deep; and the whole is then cut out and placed in a damp cellar for use.

Most potteries also possess blunging mills by which raw clay is dissolved in water, the commonest being the vaned blunger with a number of rotating vanes rotating in a tub to agitate the clay. This was then run off to be seived and evaporated.

The clay is still not ready for pottery-making, for it has to be brought to a state of plasticity by pugging. In the past, the grounding of clay into paste was done by allowing horses or barefooted men to walk on it until it was fully broken up. It is said that the puggers' feet were so sensitive that they were able to pick up the smallest pebble from the mass of clay. Later, most brickworks installed a horse-driven pug mill in the form of a gigantic coopered churn within which were a series of revolving knives. The horse, often a blind one, was hitched to a horizontal shaft and led by a young boy; it was taken round and round the churn until the contents were fully broken up and had acquired the necessary plasticity. At the present time potteries possess either a rolling mill or more commonly an oil or electrically driven pug mill. In this type of mill the clay is first tipped into a conical metal tub, where a series of revolving knives break it up; it then falls into a large drum where the pebbles and stones are separated from the clay. The clay itself is squeezed out in a spaghetti-like mass through perforations in the wall of the drum. The pure clay comes out of the mill at its lowest level in a continuous strip some twelve inches square.

Potting

The potter's ability as an artist and craftsman is exhibited most clearly in the age-old task of throwing, for he must make sure that the pots are strong yet light, and must allow for shrinkage in firing. The potter's wheel, which in itself is a very ancient piece of equipment, consists of a revolving wheel driven by foot or electric power. It must be heavy enough to revolve steadily and to ensure that the pots are symmetrical, and it must balance accurately. The thrower sits on a seat fixed to the framework of the wheel, while at the top is a tray containing the prepared balls of clay. After pressing or 'wedging', to get rid of air holes, the ball is thrown with considerable force on to the revolving disc. Wetting his hands at frequent intervals, the spinning mass is shaped into a tall cone, flattened, raised and shaped with fingers and thumb. Gradually the wall is thinned, the height is checked with a home-made gauge and the pot is removed from the wheel with the help of a wire cutter. It is then placed on a board, ready to be taken to the drying racks. At this stage the pots are described as 'green'. After drying under artificial heat or in the open air they are trimmed with a scraper as they revolve on the potter's wheel and all marks are removed with a wet sponge. Before they can be fired they have to dry out thoroughly and evenly.

Other methods of making pots are practised in some workshops, the most common being the semi-automatic process of jollying. It is particularly useful when large quantities of the same product are required. The jigger and jolly machine consists of a plaster cast of the inside of a pot firmly pegged to the revolving surface of the potter's wheel. A cast of the outside of the pot is made and carefully shaped to a metal template fixed to a movable spring arm or spreader of the machine. While the revolving plaster cast ensures the correct shape for the inside of the pot, the spreader and its template shape the outside. With a metal strike and wet sponge, they have to be cleaned on the potter's wheel. For objects of an irregular shape plaster moulds are used and the casts can be used time and time again to produce objects that are exactly the same in all details.

Green pots have to be thoroughly dried, preferably under natural conditions, before they can be fired. If they contain the slightest amount of moisture they may explode under the terrific heat of the kiln. The correct firing of pottery needs a great deal of skill, for the quality of the finished product depends as much on correct firing and keen judgment as it does on skilful throwing. The old type of kiln which may be coal, gas or wood fired, has to be carefully filled with the saggars containing green or glazed pottery. The saggars are large round or rectangular containers of coarse pottery, often made of clay and pieces of broken crockery. The heat of the kiln is raised to a very high temperature, then allowed to cool before the pots are removed.

Pottery is fired either once or twice according to the nature of the clay and the use to which the pottery is to be put. Unglazed ware and stoneware is fired only once and the products are known as 'biscuit', while most glazed ware has to be fired twice. The glaze is applied after the first firing and in the second firing it is fused with the body of the pot. Great care has to be taken in stacking glazed pottery in the kiln for no two pots must touch. In order to see what is happening inside a burning kiln, removable bricks are built into the kiln wall. Within sight inside these small peep holes are placed small, glazed fireclay cones. When their tips begin to bend over, the potter knows that the glaze is fusing and that the heat must be reduced.

Decorating and glazing

Most decoration on pottery is carried out when the clay is hard enough to handle but still soft enough to receive decoration. By far the commonest method of decoration is the application of slip, which is watered down clay in a variety of colours, sieved to remove coarse particles. This can be applied to the pottery by dipping, painting or trailed on the pot through a fine nozzle. This can be combed or inlaid on to the piece of pottery.

Glazing, whereby a chemical coating is infused over the surface of a pot, had been practised at least from medieval times, a variety of chemicals being used for this purpose. By far the most usual was galena, obtained from Derbyshire, the Mendips and the Yorkshire Dales. 'This', says Plot in 1686 'was beaten into dust, finely sifted and strewed upon them [the pots] which gives them the *gloss* but not the colour; all the colours being chiefly given by the variety of slips'.[6] Among other glazes that became increasingly popular after 1850 were ground flint, china clay, red and white lead, copper, and a variety of chemical products. Great care has to be taken in placing glazed pots in a kiln, for unless pottery is carefully stacked, the molten glaze could glue all the pottery together to make one mass.

CHAPTER SIX

Glass

Where glass is still blown by hand, methods and tools have changed but little since Roman times, and a treatise on the art of glass blowing written by Theophilus, a thirteenth-century monk, describes in detail all the techniques that would be practised in a modern glass works.

At the first hour in the morning [says Theophilus] take an iron pipe and if you wish to make sheets of glass, plunge the extremity of this pipe into a pot filled with glass. Turn the pipe in your hand until as much glass as you wish is collected round it, then taking it out put it to your mouth and blow a little; removing it immediately you put it to your cheek so as not to draw the flame into your mouth when taking breath. Keep a smooth stone also before the window [of the furnace] on which you can beat the hot glass a little, in order to give it the same thickness all over. You must alternately blow and remove the pipe with great rapidity. When it presents the form of a long hanging bladder, bring the extremity of it to the flame, the glass soon melts, and you perceive an opening. Taking a wooden tool destined for this use, give the opening the size of the centre of the glass. Afterwards join the edges together, that is to say, the upper and lower sides, in such a manner that there may be an opening on each side of the junction. Immediately touch the glass near the tube with a damp wooden instrument, shake it a little, and it will be detached. Heat the pipe in the flame of the furnace until the glass which is on it becomes liquified; place it quickly on the edges of the glass which you have united and it will adhere, take it at once and expose it to the flame of the furnace until the glass around the opening from which you have taken the pipe becomes liquid. With a round piece of wood you must dilate this opening like the preceding one; and by bringing together the edges in the middle and separating the pipe with the damp wooden tool, give it to an assistant who, introducing some wood into the opening, will carry it to the annealing oven, which should be moderately heated.

Glass is a rigid, but non-crystalline substance, usually transparent, the main constituent of which is finely ground silica, today obtained mainly from Norfolk or Loch Aline in Scotland. To act as a flux, an alkali (soda or potash) is added, while lime and other ingredients may also be included. The proportions are roughly 75 per cent silica, 15 per cent soda and 10 per cent lime, the resulting glass from this particular fusion being 'white glass', that is transparent window glass. By adding small amounts of metallic oxide a variety of colours can be produced. For example, in ancient Egypt, blue glass could be produced by adding cupric oxide and cobalt to the mixture, while Egyptian 'black glass' contains large amounts of iron, or of copper and manganese mixed.

The skilled glass-blower carries out the most delicate part of his work whilst sitting at a specially designed work-bench called a chair. The 'gaffer's chair' was evolved between 1575 and 1662 and has been regarded for centuries as one of the basic appliances of glass-making by hand. This is a low wooden bench with two parallel projecting arms each about 3 feet long. These arms are shod with steel or iron, and on them the gaffer trundles his blowing iron or pontil to preserve the circularity of the vessel as he works. He can thus rotate the pipe with his left hand, while his right hand is free to use any of the tools which hang on pegs driven into the right side of the chair. Among the most important of these tools are pucellas, tongs that resemble spring sugar tongs, that are used for shaping glass when blowing. With the pucellas, the glass blower pierces the softened end of the bubble which projects over the right arm of the chair. With one prong inside the molten glass and the other outside, the gaffer is able to squeeze the glass to the correct shape.

Traditionally, in the making of cylinder glass by hand, four men per chair are regarded as essential. These are the 'raker in' or 'boy', the junior member of the team; the 'footman' or 'servitor'; 'the gatherer', and 'the gaffer'. The blowpipe is inserted through the hole at the side of the furnace that contains the molten 'metal' and the pipe is revolved until it is coated with glass. Occasionally the pipe is withdrawn from the furnace, the glass allowed to cool slightly and then

reinserted into the furnace to gather more 'metal'. The blowpipe itself is a simple instrument, being nothing but a hollow iron or steel
pipe, 4 feet or more in length, enlarged to a knob, known as 'the nose'
at one end and tapering to a mouth piece at the other.

To gather the 'metal' the nose is heated, and when the loaded pipe
is removed from the furnace it is swung backwards and forwards with
the 'metal' hanging downwards so that it elongates. The bubble of
molten glass is then placed on the flat metal surface of the 'marver',
and marvering is completed by rolling the blowpipe from side to side
until the bubble is evenly shaped. Alternatively, the bubble may be
shaped in a rectangular metal-lined box, a process known as blocking.
Both marvering and blocking are regarded as part of the gatherer's
activity, but the actual blowing of glass is carried out by the gaffer.
The blow pipe is swung backwards and forwards; occasionally he
raises the pipe to his mouth and blows gently through the tube. The
cooling bubble has to be re-heated before being shaped on the chair,
and this is done by placing the glass in the 'glory hole' of a small furnace, usually gas fired, set near the chair. With the glass bubble on
the chair and with the pucellas in constant use the shaped vessel is
finished by being rotated against the larger flat blade of a wooden
flattening tool called 'a battledore'.

The footman or servitor then takes the pontil or punty, a solid
metal rod slightly shorter than the blow pipe, with a molten disc of
the same diameter as the cylinder on the end of the blowpipe, and
fits the molten glass disc to the cylinder on the blowpipe. With the
footman rotating the pontil and the gaffer rotating the blowpipe, the
two molten surfaces are fused together. The gaffer then breaks his
blowpipe away from the glass, leaving the glass on the pontil. The
boy removes the blowpipe and places it in a cooling rack. The rem-
nant of glass or 'moil' on the end of the pipe is removed and the pipe
is cleaned ready for use by placing it in the working hole of the furnace. The glass on the punty is again heated and is rotated as before
on one of the arms of the chair. It is the boy's task to remove glass
from the punty, by winding a thread of hot glass around the junction
of cylinder and disc. This is then touched with a cold metal rod which
fractures the glass around its circumference and, after a sharp tap, the
punty can be removed.

After cooling for approximately twelve hours, the finishing processes on glass are carried out. Formerly, the glass cylinder was placed

directly on an iron plate, but today in order to prevent scratching a flat sheet of polished glass called a 'lagre' is used. The cooled cylinder is split lengthways by a diamond tipped cutter. The cylinder is then taken to the lehr, a long flat furnace open at both ends. The glass is placed on the slowly moving conveyor belt and the heat inside the lehr increases in such a way that the glass cylinder becomes a wavy sheet of glass. The flattening is completed by means of a wooden block fixed to a long handle, known as a 'polissoir', manipulated through a small working hole into the lehr. It may take four days of carefully and critically controlled heat for the glass to travel through the lehr. The process cannot be hurried, for the glass will shatter, and careful finishing or annealing is essential.

Today very little sheet glass, except for antique glass, is made in this way, but fine quality table glass may still be largely hand blown. To make a wine-glass, for example, the gatherer takes the blow pipe, takes some molten glass from the furnace, and shapes the gather into a ball in the hollow cavity of a block. An iron mould made in two hinged halves is lined with a paste composed of resin and linseed oil, boiled together. In a chair which is working exclusively at mould-blowing, the gatherer usually does the blowing and the gaffer devotes his attention to the delicate task of shaping the glass after it has left the mould.

The blower stands on a small wooden platform over the mould, which, in turn, is over a tank of water. The platform is fitted with foot-pedals which enable the blower to open and close the mould, and to dip it into the water tank. This complete device is called a 'mechanical boy'. The blower, standing on this platform, opens the mould and lowers the pendant gather into it. When the mould is closed the blowpipe, with a moil of glass on it, rests on top. The blower rotates the pipe between his hands and blows gently into the mouthpiece. The mould is immersed in the water tank immediately before each piece is blown, so that as the gather is inflated, a steam cushion forms between the wet lining of the mould and the surface of the hot glass. The continual rotation of the pipe ensures even cooling and prevents a seam from forming at the opening of the mould. When the bowl of the glass is perfectly shaped, the blower lifts it from the mould and takes in to the chair, where the gaffer takes over.

The gaffer places the pipe across the arms of his chair and continues the rotatory movement. The footman brings the punty with a gather of glass big enough to form the stem of the wine-glass. Then the gaffer, by holding the punty with a pair of tongs, guides the gather to the bowl of the glass which is turning on the end of his blowpipe. These tongs are something like the pucellas only the blades taper to a fine point. The footman moves the punty away quickly, the added glass stretches, and the gaffer cuts off as much glass as he needs, with his shears. These shears have small blades and look rather like a pair of old-fashioned scissors. The gaffer shapes the stem by rolling and pinching the glass between the points of his tongs.

When the stem is finished, the footman brings another gather of glass on the punty and adds this to the stem so that the foot of the wine-glass can be formed; this is probably the part of his job from which the footman derives his title. The gaffer smoothes the foot to a flat disc by holding his pallette against the rotating glass.

When the base of the wine-glass is completed, the bowl must be detached from the blow-pipe in order to finish of the rim. This time the footman brings the punty with a very small gather of glass on the end. He joins this gather to the underside of the foot of the glass. The gaffer then sprinkles a few drops of water round the nose of the blow-pipe and cracks the pipe away from the bowl of the glass, which is now held by the punty. Throughout the transfer of the half-finished glass from the blowing-iron to the punty, the rotatory movement of the hot glass must be maintained; a necessity which calls for perfect coordination between the gaffer and the footman.

When the changeover has been effected, and the open end of the glass has been reheated at the glory hole, the gaffer rolls the punty up and down the arms of his chair and simultaneously trims the rim of the wine-glass with his shears. The cutting is entirely freehand, and is one of the most exacting and delicate tasks of the glass-blower. The gaffer finishes the wine-glass by a final smoothing of the rim with his pallette.

When the wine-glass is finished, the punty is broken away from the foot of the glass in the same way as the blow-pipe was, while the glass is either held in a pair of flat wooden tongs, or balanced on a broad wooden spatula. The punty always leaves a mark where it is broken away from the foot of the glass. This mark takes the form of a ring delineated by curved whirls which usually project from the base of the glass and have to be ground and polished to give an even surface. The grinding and polishing is done by pressing the glass against an abrasive wheel, which revolves on a horizontal spindle, and the final polish is given by a wheel fed with putty-powder and water. The punty mark is the sign of all handmade glasses, and the way in which the mark has been ground and polished often provides a clue as to the date of any old handmade glassware. When detached from the punty, the completed wine-glass proceeds to the final stage of the annealing lehr.

CHAPTER SEVEN

Boats

One of the most important craft industries of the past was that of boat-building, which was widely distributed along the coast and inland waterways in all parts of Britain. Many coastal and riverside villages and isolated rural districts had boatyards and the ancillary craft industries such as anchor-smithing, rope-making, sail-making and pulley-block-making that were dependent on this important maritime craft. Although boat-building and shipwrighting have declined greatly during the last hundred years, the increasing popularity of boating and yachting as recreational activities has brought new life to many a declining boatyard, and though new materials and new techniques have been introduced in recent years the methods of building wooden boats have changed hardly at all from prehistoric times. Throughout the centuries the technique of building either carvel-built boats or clinker-built boats has persisted.[1] In a carvel-built boat, a technique exemplified in early Mediterranean vessels, the side planks on the outside of the boat meet edge to edge and are secured to the frame by oak pegs (trenails or trunnells) or iron spikes. The seams of a carvel-built boat have to be thoroughly caulked to render them watertight. In clinker-built boats, developed extensively in northern Europe, the planks forming the sides of the boat are overlapped, and their overlapping edges are fastened together with clenched metal rivets.

A variety of timbers may be used in boat-building, and although in the past vast quantities of English oak were in demand by boatyards, especially for building the larger vessels,[2] today little oak is used except for occasional use in constructing keels, keelsons and stern posts. English elm, wych-elm and larch are widely used, while such timbers as mahogany and cedar are much in demand for building certain types of boat, such as those used in racing. Within recent years various laminated woods and synthetic materials, such as reinforced moulded plastics and fibreglass, have become widely employed, though a number of boat-builders still cling to traditional materials and methods of construction. In some parts of Britain, notably Scotland, larch with its natural strength and durability is still widely favoured for some parts of a boat. 'Many larches', says Edlin 'grow with a curve at the lower end of their stem, and these are prized by Scots boat-builders, since curved ribs and planking may be sawn from them, without cutting across the grain.'[3] For the sharp angled pieces, 'the knees' that hold the thwarts to the ribs of a boat, the roots of larch trees were greatly favoured until recently, again because of unbroken grain. To obtain these root-stocks 'the stump must be dug out of the ground, and one method is to fell the tree with the main roots still intact, by digging around the stump and cutting the side roots until it falls. Several knees may be sawn, or preferably cleft from each root stock, each consisting of a main side root and its proper portion of the upright trunk, some two feet long.'[4]

The boat-builder is concerned with designing the plan of a vessel, preparing the timber, organising and carrying out the construction of the boat, and launching it. Salaman points out that:

> the introduction of power saws and other machines into the shipyards took place only quite recently, 'Fifty years ago', relates a retired shipwright, Mr C. Bunday of Burleston, Hampshire, 'the only machine in the Yard was a grindstone. Everything else was done by hand.' Traditional skills in boat-building were often handed down from father to son in small family businesses, and today in many parts of the country, boatyards that have been in the same families for a century or more are often found. 'Me and my brother were apprenticed at fifteen', says a Norfolk boatbuilder . . . 'My father was a shipwright and my grandfather was a shipwright. We've always built boats, and we don't really know anything else.'[5]

The first stage in the construction of a wooden boat is the preparation of patterns, when the shape of a boat's timbers are drawn out in the mould loft. In many boat-yards, the loft has a spacious, smooth floor where the curve of a vessel's timbers are drawn full-size on the floor with chalk. In others, the drawing of the various shapes of timbers, a process known as 'laying off', is done on a large softwood board called a 'scrieve board', where the pattern of timbers is incised with a wooden handled knife with a V-shaped blade, which is used by pulling it towards the operator. This knife, known as a 'scrieve hook' is similar to a race knife used by a number of woodworkers for timber making. Scrieving on a board has an advantage over chalking on a mould-loft floor in that the markings are more permanent and may be used time and time again if the same size and shape of board is required in the future. The measuring and drawing of a boat's timbers is done with the help of 'sweeps', which are large homemade compasses and calipers. Trammells and plumb bits are also required for this vital process of laying off, while 'the curved lines are faired, that is smoothed out to the proper curve by means of thin battens, usually made of hickory, which when sprung between nails on the floor or scrieve board act as a guide'.[6]

After laying off the next step is to make the moulds or patterns from thin strips of wood, cut according to the markings on the scrieve board or mould loft floor. Since most boat-yards construct a large number of boats of the same design and size, the same patterns are used to build them all, and in most boat-yards numerous patterns hang on the walls, ready for use. These moulds are used for sawing out a boat's timber and some may be set up temporarily within the boat as a guide to the placing of timbers. Although today power-saws are used for this intricate process, a variety of saws ranging from framed pit-saws (known as a futtock, i.e. foot-hook, saw) to coarse-toothed rip saws were essential, while a ship's adze with a blade 9 inches long was an indispensable instrument for all kinds of shaping and finishing, including the trimming of curved framing and planking. The shipwright's adze, often sharpened on one side only, and the mastmaker's axe, with rounded poll for paring and trimming masts and spars, were widely used by boat-builders. To bore holes to take the trenails and bolts which held the ship together, spiral, shell and breast augers in a variety of sizes were required. Heavy metal G-cramps are used for holding the planks against the timbers to which they are attached.

Nevertheless before assembling planks and timber, the framework consisting of keel, stern post, stem and other moulded timbers are prepared. The mouldings which act as a temporary framework are attached to the keel before the planks are attached. The method of building larger sailing vessels was described as follows by G. P. B. Naish:

The keel of a new ship was laid on blocks in a dry dock and the stem-post and stern-post were erected and scarfed on to the keel at each end. This was the heaviest work. Then the floor timbers were laid across the keel; the keelson was laid along the keel on top of the floor-timbers; and the keelson, floor-timbers, and keel were bolted together. The floor-timbers were straight except at the ends, where they began to compass, that is, to turn upwards. The futtocks were next attached to the floor-timbers; these were the curved or compassing timbers that formed the curved sides of the ship. The timbers were placed very close together, and were doubled amidships and near the masts where a great strain was expected. Clamps were heavy planks running horizontally on the inside of the timbers to support the ends of the deck-beams. Partners were strong pieces of timber bolted across the deck-beams to support the masts, the heels of which were to be stepped on top of the keelson. The frame was further held together with a multitude of standing, lodging and hanging knees, all made of oak. The ship-wright always searched for crooks of timber, which he cut up most carefully to avoid waste. The elaborate construction of the bow and stern was designed to resist the straining of the rudder and the anchor-cable as well as the battering of the seas.[7]

The shape of a boat demands many bends and twists, especially near the keel, and it is usual to steam planks before nailing them in place. Trenails, which are round tough pegs of oak, are traditionally used for fastening together the parts of a boat. The best trenails are cleft rather than sawn, to ensure that no breaking takes place when they are driven in. The laying of the first planks is the most complicated of all, due to its many curves and twists. The bottom of the first plank on either side has to be riveted with copper nails both to the edge of the keel and to the stem and stern. The second plank is set to overlap the first and is riveted not only to this but also to each end. And so on right up the sides of the boat, the angle at which each plank is set always differing slightly from the ones immediately above and below it. And yet every single plank, throughout its entire length, must fit perfectly over the one below, or the boat will not be watertight.[8]

The temporary moulds around which the planks have been set in place are next removed and the permanent cross struts or ribs, care-

Fig. 5 A shipwright riveting planks

11 Oak bark for tanning, drying in the Forest of Dean

12 Leaching pits at the Colyton Tannery, Devon

13 Beam house at the Rhaedr Tannery, rebuilt at the Welsh Folk Museum

14 Currier at work at Colyton, Devon. He is using the slicker to prepare the surface of leather to receive oils

fully shaped and steamed, are put in place along the length of the boat. Then at intervals of a few inches are usually sprung into place, temporarily fixed with copper nails and finally riveted.

Caulking a boat is a process that calls for special skills and special tools. Fantailed chisels with either sharp or blunt edges and provided with grooves, known as creases, are used for driving in the strands of oakum into the seams between the planks. In a clinker-built boat, caulking is not necessary and a coat of lead paint makes the boat waterproof. In a carvel-built boat, however, all the seams have to be caulked. The seam is first opened with a reaming iron, a wedge-shaped chisel with a 3 inch blade, and the threads of oakum are driven in with a caulking iron, a wooden beetle being used for hammering the chisel head. The oakum is further compressed ('hardened down') and sunk below the surface with a making iron. This has a ground blade and is essential to leave sufficient room between the planks for the subsequent insertion of pitch. Caulking was usually done left to right: 'hardening down' from right to left. 'Much experience and skill was needed to judge how much oakum should be forced into the seam; too little would not keep the water out, but too much could spring the planks apart and even shear off a bolt or trenail.'[9]

The main body of the boat is now complete, but there are still a number of tasks to be undertaken. The keelson has to be shaped and fitted. This is a 'kind of second keel' that the boat builder 'bolts securely over the top of the timbers to the keel below'.[10] He also has to fasten the three stringers, 'bilge', 'rising' and 'gunwale' stringers that are attached all round the inside of the boat to give added strength.

CHAPTER EIGHT

Leather

Tanning

Tanning is a chemical process concerned with the conversion of the gelatinous part of the skin, known as the dermis or corium, into leather, by impregnating it with tannic acid. Raw skin, stiff as a board when dry, can be dissolved in water, whereas tanned leather can be repeatedly wetted and dried without changing its character in any way. The corium is the central layer in an animal skin and it is composed 'of long, fine collagen fibrils of which twenty to fifty are grouped together to form fibres. These, in turn, are grouped into bundles bound by netlike or reticular tissue. Thus the corium is a complex substance of great strength and flexibility.'[1] In the tanning process, it is this central layer of fibres that has to be preserved, for the layer above it—the epidermis with the hair or wool growing from it has to be removed, as has the subcutaneous layer of tissue, fat and flesh below the corium. Both these processes, of unhairing and fleshing, were carried out by craftsmen known as 'beamsmen' near, or in, the beam house on the south side of the tan yard.

There are three basic ways of turning skin into leather.[2] They are:

1. *Chamoising*. This process, which dates back to prehistoric times, consists of working greasy and albuminous substances of fish oils and animal fats into the skins. The surface of the skin was scraped to facilitate absorption and the skin had to be strained and pulled out in all directions so that the oils penetrated it completely. The skins were then placed in a warm room and oxidation took place. The leather produced by this technique was flexible, tough and pale yellow in colour.

2. *Tawing*. This is another method that dates back to prehistoric times and it consisted of applying alum and salt to a raw hide. In time, this produced a pure white leather, which had to be softened by rub-

bing or 'staking' against a blunt edge. Despite its popularity, especially for making gloves, tawed leather was not stable, for it could
be reconstituted into the basic elements and was therefore not true
leather.

3. *Vegetable tanning*. This was by far the most common method of
tanning in post-medieval times. In this process, animal pelts were
preserved by employing the chemical process of tanning. Tannin is
present in a wide range of vegetable matter, but the commonest
source was oak bark obtained preferably from twenty-five or thirty-
year-old coppice oak. This was ground in a bark mill and mixed with
cold water to produce the tanning liquor. This was the method of
tanning used in most Welsh, heavy-leather tanneries and it is the
process still carried out at such tanneries as Colyton, Devon, and
Grampound, Cornwall.

Raw material

The heavy leather tanneries were mainly concerned with producing
leather for boot uppers and soles, harness, strong straps and other
purposes and obtained hides from a variety of sources. Until the last
quarter of the nineteenth century the main suppliers were the butchers. Hides were collected regularly from the numerous slaughter-
houses of a region, although in most cases by 1880, the local supply
of hides had dwindled. The tanneries became more and more dependent on hide markets in industrial cities for their supplies. Imported
hides, dried or salted, were also widely used.

The principal categories of skins used at the tannery were:

Hides. The skins of larger, fully-grown animals such as bulls, cows,
oxen, horses, buffaloes and hippopotami. Hides were mainly used for
making heavy harness leather and sole leather. Hides could be sub-
divided again into:

(a) Slaughter, market or green hides from the abattoirs of Britain.
These varied greatly in substance, size and texture, Scotch
hides being particularly favoured by mid-Wales craftsmen.

(b) Dried hides imported mainly from Argentina and Uruguay.
They were also known as 'flint hides' and since they were as

hard as horn they had to be soaked in water for some hours and then rubbed and beaten before tanning.

(c) Dried salted hides imported mainly from the West Indies, Brazil and South Africa. Before they could be tanned all traces of salt had to be removed.

(d) Wet salted hides, many of them from Australia and the Baltic regions arrived at the tannery, tightly packed in casks containing brine. Again all traces of salt had to be removed before liming and tanning.

Kips. These were the skins of the younger of the large animals, such as the skins of heifers, younger oxen and horses. The leather derived from these skins was usually thinner, more supple and of better grain than the hides and it could be used for such purposes as making boot and shoe upper leather. Again they could be market kips, dried, salted or brined kips.

Skins. Those of smaller animals such as sheep, goats, pigs and seals. These were not as important at the Rhaeadr tannery (Radnorshire) as heavy leathers, although small quantities were processed, particularly during the present century. The Rhaeadr tannery has been re-erected at the Welsh Folk Museum, near Cardiff. (See Gazetteer). Skins were used for such things as boot uppers, gloves, upholstery, book bindings, seats of saddles and for all other purposes where soft leather was required. The tanyards still in production in Wales, as at Llanidloes, Newtown, Caerffili, Llandeilo and Dolgellau are really skin yards, where only light sheep and goat skins are processed.

Preliminary operations

The first process in the lengthy business of tanning was to cleanse each hide in the water-pit in front of the beam house. All traces of salt had to be removed from imported hides while dry hides had to be made supple by frequent soaking and scrubbing. In the case of market hides, it was vital that all traces of blood were removed, as the presence of blood in leather leaves a dark stain and poor grain. At many Welsh tanneries, it was customary to keep one or two large mastiff dogs, and it is said that as soon as market hides were delivered to the tannery, each one was pegged to the ground so that the dogs could bite off any fats or flesh that adhered to the skins. The mastiffs were useful to guard the premises and to keep under control the vast numbers of rats that always infested tanneries. In addition, the dogs' excreta, when mixed with hot water, was essential for treating certain types of soft leather before tanning.

Occasionally market hides could not be used immediately and in order to prevent putrefaction they were salted and kept for a few days. The cleaning of hides was carried out in the water-pit immediately in front of the beam house. This measured 7 feet square and received a constant supply of clean water. The presence of an overflow pipe ensured a gentle movement of the water. Many tanners believed that the best way to clean market hides was to place them for some hours in a swiftly flowing stream. In addition to removing impurities, the water bath had the effect of swelling up the fibres of the hide, bringing them back as near as possible to the condition in which they left the animals' backs. Hides were usually left in the water pit for a week or so, but since the water was seldom changed, it was 'full of putrefaction bacteria, the action of which assisted the softening . . . at the cost of a serious loss of valuable hide substance'.[2] When market hides were particularly dirty, they had to be removed from the water pit and scraped with a blunt two-handled draw knife, somewhat similar to the striking pin used at a later stage in leather manufacture.

Unhairing and fleshing

The craftsman responsible for the tasks of unhairing and fleshing was known as 'a beamsman' and he worked in a building known as a 'beam house'. At the Rhaeadr tannery, the beam house, with its three pits and wide doors and shutters, was especially designed for what must have been the most unhealthy and unpleasant tasks in the tannery. The beam, from which the workshop and the craftsmen took their names, is a working table or horse, with a convex or steeply sloping surface of iron or wood. The hide was thrown over this for unhairing and fleshing.

Before the hides were taken to the beam house, however, they were placed in one of the three lime pits in order to loosen the epidermis and the fats and flesh that adhered to the corium or true skin. Slaked lime was mixed with water in varied proportions and placed in the pits. The first pit, in which hides were soaked for a day or two, contained a weak mixture of lime, very often a weak solution of old lime, highly charged with bacteria. The second pit contained a less mellow but a slightly stronger mixture, while the third contained a strong solution of new lime. The hides remained in the pits until the hair was easily removed, but the length of liming depended partly on the quality of leather required; the softer the leather, the longer the hide remained in the pit and the mellower the solution. For example, hides designed for sole leather had to be hard and tough and eight or ten days in strong lime was sufficient. Harness leather, on the other hand, which had to be much more pliable, required mellow liming of twelve to fourteen days, while soft shoe upper leather required anything up to six weeks in weak, mellow lime. The skins were either suspended by chains from the iron bars at the side of the pits or allowed to float in the lime solution.

With the tanner's hook, the hides were removed from the lime pits and placed over the beam, flesh side inwards. The beamsmen then took the blunt-bladed, unhairing knife, curved to fit the convex surface of the beam. The hair was easily removed by pressing the knife downwards against the hides. It was important not only to remove the hair but also most of the hair root sheaths, which could discolour the finished leather. The hair was not thrown away but was sold to plasterers and stone masons as an essential constituent of mortar. Some also went to upholsterers and to manufacturers of cheap clothing.

The fleshing operation was much more skilled than that of unhairing, for the flesh had to be removed in such a way as not to damage the true skin in any way. The slightest deviation of the knife could make a hide completely useless. The flesh was shaved away with a very sharp double-edged, two-handled knife. The concave edge was used for scraping, the convex for cutting. Fleshings and other matters cut away at this stage were thrown into a pit. The fleshings were then taken away for making glue and gelatine.

After unhairing and fleshing, the pelts were thoroughly washed, and the heavier hides were again placed over the beam and the remaining lime squeezed out with a blunt curved knife called a 'scudder'. This usually had a slate blade. After thorough washing and 'raising' in a weak acid solution, the heavy hides were ready for the tanning process itself. Lighter hides for making soft leather, such as those of calves, seals and sheep, were not washed after unhairing and fleshing, neither were they scudded. The 'slitters', as they were called, were thrown into one of the three pits at the back of the beam house. These were the 'mastering pits' and they contained a mixture of either hen or pigeon dung and cold water; a mixture known as 'bates'; or a mixture of warm water and dog excreta known as a 'pure' or 'drench'. The acid liquor of the mastering pits removed the lime, without any danger of damaging the pelt by scudding. Great care had to be taken not to leave the pelts in the mastering pits for too long as the solution would rapidly reduce the substance of the hides. In the case of bates, skins were immersed for a period of ten to twelve days, but a few hours was sufficient in a drench. The slitters were again thoroughly washed in the water-pit before tanning.

Rounding

Before a hide is tanned, it has to be divided into several parts; a process known as 'rounding'. The reason for this is that a hide contains several qualities of skin, so that if a complete hide were immersed in the tanning liquor, the coarse-grained and open-pored offal would absorb the best tannin. The rounding table at the Rhaeadr tannery was an ordinary wooden trestle table, 60 inches long and 30 inches wide. On this a hide was rounded with a sharp butcher's knife. The cheeks, the most inferior part of the hide, were first removed, then the shoulders or forepart, and the two sides of the bellies, leaving the thickest and best part of the hide, known as the 'butt'. At the end of the tanning process the butt could be divided into two sections known as 'bends', which could be used for the best quality sole and harness leather. Hides were again washed, occasionally in a weak solution of boracic acid and were then ready for the actual tanning.

Leaching

To make tanning liquor, the craftsman needed a vast quantity of oak bark, ground finely and mixed with cold water in the so-called 'leaching pits'. In the past, oak was especially grown in coppices and the bark was harvested after some twenty-five or thirty-years' growth. The coppicing of oak trees for bark was an extremely expensive process, for vast quantities of bark were required by every tannery. Some eighteenth-century mid-Wales farmers regarded the production of oak bark as an essential part of the farm economy and the demand for good quality oak bark at that time was large indeed.

In more recent times bark was obtained as a byproduct of winter-felled oak trees or those felled during the spring months. It was far easier to remove the bark from spring-felled oak. A tree is scored at regular intervals of some 24 inches with a bark knife. Vertical slits are then made and large semicylindrical plates of bark are levered off. As tannin is soluble in water, the plates of bark have to be stacked in such a way that rain does not penetrate into the stack. Barking was a task often undertaken by women and children, who sold the bark to the tanneries, and the oaks of central Wales and Herefordshire were considered especially rich in tannin.

One of the most unpopular tasks at a tannery was that of grinding oak bark, for the fine dust emanating from the water-driven bark mill penetrated everywhere. The large dried plates of oak bark were taken to the loft above the mill and fed into the hopper of the grinder. The plates were pushed down between the rapidly revolving cutters of the mill. The bark shed itself at the Rhaeadr factory is a large, high building which in the heyday of tanning was kept full of ground and unground bark, collected from the forests of mid-Wales and the border counties. Slits in the south wall ensured adequate draughts, so that the plates of bark were thoroughly dried before grinding.

The ground bark was carried from the mill in large baskets to the leaching pits where the tanning liquor was made by adding cold water to the bark, and allowing the mixture to stand for some weeks before use. The tanning liquor in various strengths was then pumped to the tan pits proper.

Suspending, handling and laying

The method of tanning heavy hides consisted of the progression of butts through a series of pits, possibly numbering ten or more, containing liquors of varying strengths, starting with the weakest solutions. The first series are the suspenders, and in these pits containing the weakest solution in the tannery, the butts were first placed. Each hide was attached to a string which was tied to sticks laid across the top of the pit. The object of suspending was to ensure the uniform absorption of tannin by the pelts when they were transferred to stronger solutions at a later stage. The liquor in the suspender pits was stirred gently at frequent intervals, and the hides were moved daily from one suspender to the other; the liquors becoming progressively stronger from one pit to the next. The tanner had to be very careful that the hides did not touch one another in the suspender pit, or they would display touch marks and be of uneven colour.

At the end of the suspender stage the butts, with all traces of lime removed, would be soft and porous, and they had to be laid flat to straighten out creases, before being placed in the next set of pits—the handlers or floaters. Here the hides were laid flat rather than suspended and were moved from one pit to the other at regular intervals of two or three days. The twelve handlers at the Rhaeadr tannery contained progressively stronger liquors. During the first two or three days of handling hides were turned over in the liquor with the aid of tanning hooks at least twice a day so that the the liquor penetrated the hide fully. A bucketful of finely ground oak bark was often added to the tanning liquor in the last three or four handlers, while in some cases bark was sprinkled evenly on the hides before they were immersed in the pits. The handling of butts took from six to eight weeks, but at this stage only about a third of the substance of each hide had been fully tanned. To distribute bark evenly throughout the pit, a long handled wooden plunger was used while hides were moved from one handling pit to the other by means of long-handled tongs or hooks.

The spent liquors in the first two or three handlers were then pumped back to the suspenders and new, stronger liquors pumped to the last handling pits. The hides were then passed to the final set of pits, the layers, which contained the strongest liquors in the yard. Each hide was sprinkled with oak bark to a depth of about one inch. Bark was first spread on the bottom of the pit and a butt placed over it. This was followed by another layer of bark, then a butt until the pit was tightly packed. Tanning liquor from the leaching pits was then pumped into the layer pits. The butts were left undisturbed in the first layer pit for some six weeks until the tannin and animal fibre had combined. The butts were then taken out, stratified with bark again and placed in the second layer pit, containing a stronger solution of tanning liquor. Depending on the thickness of the hide, the process of laying could go on for as long as eighteen months; indeed occasionally hides were laid away for as long as three years before they were fully tanned.

Drying

After removal from the layer pits, the fully tanned hides were washed in a weak solution of tanning liquor and any particles of tanning materials that still adhered to the pelt were brushed off with a stiff brush. In some cases the wet hides were placed over the wooden horse, which may be seen against the east wall of the drying room, and the bloom removed with the striking pin. This is a three-bladed triangular draw knife and it was pressed firmly over the grain side of the hide until all traces of tanning liquor had been removed. In other cases the wet hide was placed on the stone scouring table in the centre of the yard and the bloom from the grain side removed with a piece of stone called 'a scouring stone'. The grain was wiped with a cloth and a thin coating of linseed or cod liver oil was applied over the grain surface of the leather to prevent the too rapid drying of the surface.

The process of drying itself demanded considerable care, for if the drying were too slow a mould would grow on the tanned hide. If, on the other hand, the drying were too quick, the leather would be discoloured, hard and brittle. The drying room with adjustable wooden weatherboards ensured good ventilation and the gentle movement of air currents to dry the hides as they hung from the racks. Unfortunately the drying room was also very dark: it was extremely important that the hides should not be subjected to direct sunlight, as this too could damage the texture and colour of leather. After the skins had been partially dried, perhaps for a week or ten days, they were taken down from the drying racks, damped and piled in heaps, with sacks between each hide. This was the process of 'samming' or tempering the hides to a moist and uniformly soft condition. They were then submitted again to the process of striking with the pin and then rolled. The roller consists of a brass cylinder surmounted by a heavily weighted box truck and a long wooden handle. The butt was laid flat on the solid and level wooden bed, coated with sheets of zinc, and the roller was passed over the butt repeatedly until the creases had been removed. After the first rolling the butt was again hung for some days, it was re-oiled and rolled. This process of oiling the flesh and grain side, rolling and drying, could be repeated a number of times. After thorough drying the tanner's work was complete, but before a piece of tanned leather could be sold to the bootmakers, saddlers and other craftsmen, it had to pass through the hands of another craftsman, the currier.

Of course, there were considerable differences in tanning between the various categories of hides. The above description was the general method adopted for processing cattle butts for sole leather. Sole leather could be finished by the tanners by rollers and oiling, but other types had to be sent to the currier for finishing.

The Rhaeadr tannery did of course produce other types of leather. Harness and shoe upper leather for example were washed, limed, fleshed and unhaired in the same way as for sole leather, but it was essential that all traces of lime were removed before tanning. The lighter variety of supple hides were bated in hen manure and then placed in the suspender and handler pits for two months or so, in a very weak solution of tanning liquor. Most of the hides remained in the layer pits for eight months, but on drying they were not subjected to the repeated heavy rollings of the sole leather, but were sent to the currier for dressing. Soft leathers, especially for shoe uppers, were usually made more supple by rubbing them against the knife of a 'stake'. This is a metal blade attached to an upright piece of wood, and alumed horse leather in particular had to be rubbed against this for a considerable period before it was ready for dressing.

At Rhaeadr, Colyton and Grampound, although oak bark was the main tanning agent used, after the mid-nineteenth century other agents of vegetable and chemical origins were added. Some of the tans helped the tanning process and vegetable matters such as sumac (the shoots and leaves of a Mediterranean tree), quebracho (a South American timber) and valonia (acorn cups from Mediterranean oaks) were often added to the oak bark, particularly after 1860. Non-tans in the form of chemical elements were also added occasionally, and although these did not tan the hides, they served a useful purpose in that they slowed down the rate of tanning, enabling the tans themselves to penetrate right through the hide.

Currying

While the tanner's craft was one that demanded considerable knowledge of chemical processes, that of the currier demanded a high degree of skill in the use of hand tools that are entirely different from those used by any other leather worker. Currying is to a large extent a mechanical operation; cleansing, reducing in thickness and softening the leather and the impregnation with oil and fats. The tanner could not complete his work of producing supple leather of good appearance, without the assistance of the currier, for although the finishing employed by the tanner may be good enough for hard, stiff sole leather, it is certainly not good enough for harness and shoe upper leather, where good appearances and suppleness are important.

It was formerly illegal to carry on together the two trades of tanning and currying; and thus two operations, which were naturally part of the same process, became separated, and leather was dried out by the tanner to be wetted again by the currier, instead of proceeding at once to curry the wet leather.

Currying is a lengthy and complex process and the methods of working depend very largely on the type of leather required. The currier has to produce leathers of different weights, grades, colours and suppleness, by the use of a variety of oils and greases and the use of a wide range of hand tools.

After delivery from the tanners, the currier's first task was to prepare the leather for dyeing or polishing, by removing the 'bloom' and the tried tanning liquor that clogged up the grain. The hide was soaked and softened in water or in a hot sumac bath. It was then either laid on the stone scouring table in the centre of the yard or on the slate table in the cellar for scouring. Both tables have a slight inclination so that the hot water, brushed on in ample quantities with a hard brush, ran off. To scrape the bloom from leather, a variety of wooden handled slickers or stretching irons were used. A slicker has a flat steel blade measuring 6 inches wide and 4 inches deep, set in a wooden handle. In some cases, copper or stone bladed slickers were preferred, but they were not sharpened in any way as this could damage the delicate surface of the leather. For horse hides and other light coloured leathers, copper slickers were always used as iron or steel blades could easily blemish the surface of the white leather.

After scouring and slicking the hides were partially dried or 'sammed', and then shaved or split. The shaving of hides was the most complex of all processes in leather production and it demanded considerable dexterity. The operation was carried out on the wooden beam, which may be seen on the left hand side of the mahogany currying table. The beam consists of a stout square of wood on which the currier stood, and into one end of this a strong, hard-wood plank was fixed at an angle of eighty degrees. The working surface is formed by a very smooth piece of lignum vitae attached to the upright. Beams varied in size according to the height and preferences of the currier and it was customary for each currier to have his own beam, specially constructed and adjusted to suit him.

The currier's knife is a heavy rectangular, double-edged tool made of fine steel, held by a bar down the centre, with a handle at each end. One handle is horizontal and the other, usually held in the currier's left hand, is vertical. In the early nineteenth century, Cirencester was the centre for the manufacturing of these peculiarly shaped knives. Sharpening a currier's knife demanded great skill for first of all it had to be sharpened with a rubstone and this was followed by rubbing with the clearing stone, until all the scratches of the rubstone disappeared. The knife was then placed between the craftsman's knees with the straight handle and one end of the cross handle resting on the ground. The edge was they gradually turned over at right angles to the blade by rubbing with a smooth steel held in both hands. The knife had to be resharpened repeatedly, using a small, wooden handled steel, almost like a knitting needle, which was passed over the edge, first outside and then down the angle formed by turning.

The process of shaving and skiving was carried out on the flesh side of the hide, and this operation required considerable skill and precision to prevent the knife from cutting too deeply into the surface of the leather.

Certain kinds of leather were subjected to the process of stoning before they were flattened, the craftsman using a stone-bladed slicker or stockstone passed over the grain side of the leather for this process. In this process the grain was smoothed and the leather stretched. The slicker or stretching iron used at this stage of the work is a plate of iron or steel, set in a wooden handle and sharpened with a rubstone. The scraping blade has a turned edge and in operation skins were placed in water and then laid flat on the table, grain side downward and the flesh side rubbed with the slicker. Usually two men working from either side of the skin were engaged in slicking, scraping away particles of leather. The grain adhered firmly to the surface of the table and a hard brush with a plentiful supply of water was used for cleaning away the particles of scraped leather. The bloom on the surface of the leather, which had the appearance of a white film, was removed with stockstone and scouring brush, pumice stone and glass slicker, after which the leather was oiled and placed in the drying loft to harden.

The next stage in the processing of leather consisted of brushing its surface with dubbing; a process known as 'stuffing'. The dubbing used at most tanneries was made up of equal quantities of tallow and cod oil. In mid-Wales tallow from Welsh mountain sheep, whose grease was regarded as far more suitable for making dubbing than that obtained from lowland sheep was used for stuffing. The cod oil was usually imported in large casks from Newfoundland. Occasionally, 'sod oil', a greasy substance obtained in the treatment of sheep skins, was added to the dubbing. At the stuffing stage, the hides had to be slightly moist and the dubbing could be applied to one or both surfaces of the leather. A hard, round brush was used for applying a thick coat of the oil and the hides were then allowed to dry slowly for some weeks. As the water in the hide evaporated, its place was taken by the liquid part of the dubbing, becoming thoroughly distributed over its surface. The harder fats, known as 'table grease' was left on the surface of the leather and it was afterwards removed by slicking. In a modern tannery, stuffing is completed in a revolving drum.

The surplus grease on the surface of the leather had to be removed after drying with a 'whitening slicker'. Whitening was performed on a sheet of framed plate glass 3 feet long by 2 feet wide placed on the table, and the whitening slicker, like the currier's knife, has a turned edge that constantly needs turning with the steel. Usually only the flesh side of a hide was whitened, but occasionally a thin film of the grain, if it was marked in any way, had to be slicked. This process was known as 'buffing'. The finishing processes differed considerably according to the types of leather produced. For some leathers, a grained effect was required, and this was obtained by rubbing a cork board, usually a convex soled tool 9 inches long and 4 inches wide attached to the worker's forearm by a leather strap. First the leather was boarded lengthways, then across and finally from corner to corner, to that a pebbled grain of no definite form resulted. This process also softened the leather.

In some cases the flesh side of a hide had to be blackened and a mixture of lamp black and soap was applied to it. This was followed by a solution of size, prepared by boiling glue in water which after drying was smoothed and brightened by glassing or rubbing with a thick, smooth glass slicker. When leather had to be blacked on the grain side, for example harness leather, a mixture of ferrous sulphate and logwood was brushed on it. The leather had to be prepared first by brushing it over with urine or a solution of soda in water. After applying the dyeing solution the skin was placed grain side on the table and the flesh side shaved with a sharp slicker. It was then turned over again and rubbed with tallow, and finally rubbed with a blunt steel slicker, mahogany board and, according to experienced curriers, with the bare forearm which gave the black leather a sheen.

In finishing calf leather, widely used for making shoe uppers, the grain side was oiled before stuffing and the flesh side was slicked. Cork was required for raising the grain very slightly and after gentle slicking of both the flesh and grain side, lamp black was applied to the flesh side. This surface was then glassed a number of times before the skin was cut up ready for use.

CHAPTER NINE

Clogs and Boots

Clogs

Until fairly recent times every town, village and country district had its complement of craftsmen able to make footwear for the local community. In many parts of the country, especially in Wales and the North of England, clogs were the universal footwear and they remained so until recently amongst textile workers, miners and farmworkers. The clog is still widely worn in steel works and on wet factory floors, while specially insulated clogs are worn by electricity workers.

The origin of the clog is lost in the mists of antiquity, but clogs were certainly worn by rich and poor alike in the Middle Ages. Their great advantage over other types of footwear is the fact that they are warm and perfectly waterproof in all conditions. The thick wooden soles and iron rims keep the wearer's feet well above the level of a wet factory or dairy floor, while in muddy fields they are ideal. In theory at least, each clog is a perfect fit for the wearer, for the craftsman makes his clogs according to the shape, size and peculiarities of each person's feet. At least this was the case when the village or town clogmaker was concerned with supplying his local community with footwear, although this type of craftsman is a rarity today.

In the heyday of the clog there were three distinct types of craftsman concerned in the clog-making industry.

1. The village or town clog-maker concerned with supplying a local market. He made clogs for each individual buyer and since he was responsible for making the whole clog with hand tools, his trade demanded a considerable knowledge, not only of leatherwork, but of woodwork as well.

2. The clog sole cutter or clogger, who was in the past very often an itinerant craftsman undertaking no work but the cutting and rough

74

15 A battery of lime pits. After washing and soaking the hides are suspended in saturated lime solution with the addition of sodium sulphide. This is an aid to hair removal

16 Splitting the hide. This follows the washing, liming and fleshing. A very technical and precise operation. The top or outer grain is the one from which upholstery leather is made. The bottom or flesh split is used for the manufacture of suede leathers

17 A bootmaker at Long Buckby, Northants

18 A country clog maker. Thomas James of Solva, Pembrokeshire using a clogger's knife

shaping of alder or beech blocks for clogging factories. In addition to travelling cloggers, there were also clog sole factories, such as one that still operates in the West Riding town of Hebden Bridge, where clog soles, often of imported timber, are cut on machines in readiness for use in clog-making factories.

3. Clog making factories employing a number of people where clog soles and uppers are shaped and assembled. The principal factories that have persisted to this day are at Huddersfield and Halifax in Yorkshire and at Rossendale and St Helens in Lancashire.

The itinerant clogger or clog sole maker was concerned only with the rough shaping of wooden soles which were sold to the clogging factories of Lancashire and Yorkshire. It was one of the most picturesque of all the rural crafts, but it has almost certainly disappeared completely from all parts of Britain. Before 1939, clogging gangs were a very common sight in all parts of Britain, but the alder groves of South Wales and the Border counties were particularly well known as their haunt. Like the Buckinghamshire chair bodger and the Dorset hurdle-maker, the clogger represented an age-old tradition of craftsmanship; craftsmen who found it easier to take their few simple tools to the forests rather than take timber, often from inaccessible coppices, to a permanent village workshop.

For clog sole making the craftsman requires a timber that does not split easily, but on the other hand, it must be relatively easy to shape. As clogs are used on wet factory floors, mines and muddy fields, the sole must be durable in water and completely waterproof. Tough, resilient willow which lasts indefinitely in moist conditions is occasionally used by north country craftsmen as is birch and beech, but in that area as well as in Wales nearly all the clogs are equipped with alder or sycamore soles. While many village clogmakers use sycamore, the itinerant cloggers, by tradition are craftsmen in alder. Alder, a riverside tree, grows best in good fertile soil, with running water near the roots. It grows profusely in favoured conditions, its seed being carried from one place to the other by the streams. The timber it produces is soft and perishable under ordinary conditions, for it contains a great deal of moisture. In wet places, however, it is extremely durable and for this reason alder is widely used for such specialised tasks as reveting river banks. It can only be harvested in the spring and summer months and must be left to season for at least nine months before it can be used. Clogging was therefore a seasonal occupation and gangs of a dozen or more craftsmen wandered from grove to grove, living a hard, tough life in roughly built temporary shelters. In Wales the clogger reckoned that the amount of money made from selling waste material as pea-sticks and firewood should be enough to buy all the food the gang needed while they worked in the woods.

After felling alder trees no more than 24 inches in girth, the clogger sawed the trunks into logs of fixed lengths, of four sizes— men's, women's, middles and children's. Each log was then split with a beetle and wedge or with axe and mallet into blocks, which were cut with the clogger's knife into the rough shape and sizes of the clog soles. This process was known as 'breaking up'. If the alder trees used were small nine-year coppice trees, their girth would be considerably smaller, and the splitting process with beetle and wedge was un- necessary.

The work with the clogger's stock knife was highly skilled and intricate. The knife itself is made of one piece of steel, some 30 inches in length, bent to an obtuse angle in the middle. The blade is some 4 inches deep and 13 inches long and the whole knife terminates in a hook. This hook was fastened to a ring on a wooden post driven firmly into the ground and forming one of the supports of a low bench. The clogger grasped the wooden handle, which is at right angles to the shank, while with his left hand an alder billet, resting on the bench and moving it as required. The large clogger's knife known as a 'bench' or 'paring knife', is still produced by some large- scale manufacturers, and with its stout hook and long handle it gives play to the craftsman who wishes to make rapid cuts at different angles. As such it is still used for some purposes in factories along with a variety of modern machinery. The clogger, stooping over the knife, cut an alder billet into the rough shape of a sole with great certainty and speed. A deep notch was cut in the block at a point where heel and sole were designed to meet, and the clog blocks were built into small conical stacks. These stacks, which had to re- main in the open air for some weeks if not months, were built in such a way that air could circulate freely between the blocks to hasten the drying process, for 'breaking up' was undertaken while the timber was still green and moist. The rough blocks were then sent to north country clog factories where they were finally shaped in workshops.

In some parts of the country one craftsman was responsible for making both clogs and boots. In others the clogmaker was a specialised craftsman, concerned only with making wooden-soled clogs. In addition to itinerant cloggers, almost every village and rural locality, particularly in the north and west, had its clogmaker, who made footwear for each individual buyer, measuring the feet and making clogs to fit. Unlike the clogger, the village craftsman used a great deal of sycamore. In the past Welsh clogmakers reckoned that a sycamore tree cut from the hedgerow produced far superior soles to those cut from a forest or plantation. The trees are felled and immediately converted into sole blocks; first with beetle and wedge, then with an axe, and finally with the large stock knife. The process so far is similar to that adopted by itinerant cloggers, and a few deft strokes with this guillotine-like stock knife soon reduces the blocks of wood to nearly the correct shape. In the case of the village clogmaker, however, measurements that are more accurate than the cloggers men's, women's, middles and children's are adopted, for the clogmaker measures the customer's feet accurately and transfers those measurements to a paper pattern. In many clogmaker's workshops, patterns representing the feet of generations of local inhabitants may still be found. After highly skilled work with the stock knife, a similar knife, but in this case with a convex blade some three inches wide is used to shape the top surface. This is the hollowing knife and it is followed by the morticing knife or gripper, whose narrow V-shaped blade cuts a channel for fitting the leather uppers all round the sole. Finally the sole is finished with rasps and short-bladed knives until it is perfectly smooth.

The leather uppers are again cut out in accordance with a paper pattern, the method of working being the same as clicking in bootmaking. Stiffeners are inserted at the heels, lace holes are cut and eyelets fitted and the assembled leather uppers are strained over a wooden last. It is tacked in place, hammered into shape and left in the last for a few hours to be moulded into the correct shape. Unlike a boot, the clog is removed from the last before assembling and the clog upper is not sewn to the sole, but nailed with short flat-headed nails. A narrow strip of leather is cut and placed over the junction of uppers and sole. Great care has to be taken to ensure that the nails used in assembling point downwards and are in no danger of damaging the wearer's feet. Replaceable grooved irons are nailed to the sole and heel; a bright copper or brass tip is tacked to the front and the clogs are ready for wear. With constant use and the replacement of irons at regular intervals, a pair of clogs may last without resoling for at least twelve years.

Typical of the clog-making factories that were once common in Lancashire and Yorkshire are the premises of F. Walkley at Birkly, Huddersfield, where fourteen people are employed, most of them on piecework. The clogs they make are specialised ones for industry; some are insulated for use by workers walking across the top of electric furnaces, others are lined with felt for use by workers in cold and wet conditions, as in breweries. In addition to new leather, most of it from Northamptonshire tanneries, leather impregnated with oils originally used in condensing machinery in wool carding mills is in considerable demand. Not only is this leather waterproof, but it is also considerably cheaper than new leather.

The making of clogs is divided into three processes, a group of craftsmen being responsible for each. First is the clicking section where a large room is devoted to the cutting of the leather uppers. Incidentally, the wooden soles are obtained from a specialised clog sole cutter at Hebden Bridge, for rarely were the clog-making factories responsible for the shaping of soles. The word 'clicking' is derived from the fact that as leather was cut by hand on a compressed wooden board it made a peculiar clicking sound. Nowadays hand-cutting to a pattern is rarely undertaken and leather is clicked by means of electrically driven presses that carry especially shaped steel cutters. All the various sections of the clog uppers are cut in this way. Occasionally, however, leather is still cut by hand, if for instance, the clogs to be made are particularly large. The patterns in this case are usually of thick cardboard or of thinner cardboard with a metal edging. The clicking board itself is of compressed wood 34 in by 16 in and 3·5 in thick, is springy and the nature of the board will not damage the sharp edge of the short-bladed clicking knife. The secret of clicking lies in the fact that the craftsman is able to cut up the leather in such a way that there is very little wastage.

The second section of the clog-making factory consists of the closing shop, where the various parts of the clog upper are stitched together. Traditionally this is women's work, and sewing machines are used for closing. The component parts of a clog are brought in from the clicking room in stacks, each marked with its size in chalk. The components are placed on a table in the centre of the workshop, the size number is stamped on, lace hole eyelets are cut and a line is scored along the surface of the leather to indicate the position of stitching. Stitching the various parts of the clogs—tongues, fronts, backs, toe caps and linings—is carried out with considerable speed but due to the complexity of sewing some of the more specialised clogs, the women employed in the closing room are often paid on a time, rather than a piece work basis.

There are six men employed in the assembling room, five assembling clogs and one attaching rubber soles to the clogs. The assemblers are paid according to the number of pairs of clogs turned out—they receive anything from 50p to £2.10 per dozen pairs of clogs according to the type produced. Therefore, they are virtually able to work their own hours, but probably in the region of 8 to 8½ hours a day. Each man assembles about 4 to 5 dozen pairs a day, taking approximately ten minutes to assemble a pair, thus a thousand or more pairs of clogs are assembled in one week in the factory.

The clogmaker is seated with a 'stithy' (a metal horse for holding the clog in place) between the knees, feet on the circular base. The sole and heel irons are nailed on to the wooden sole, which is resting on the stithy, using the ironing hammer and tip nails—blunt ended nails with rectangular flat heads and rectangular in shape. Square or rectangular nails are used so as not to split the wood and are inserted at an angle. Using a stamp, the assembler applies his initials to the clog sole.

Finally comes the lasting process. The leather upper is nailed to the sole at the very back of the heel with one nail. The wooden last is then placed on the sole and the leather upper stretched over the last ready to be nailed down. The clog is held between the knees. The inner leather toe-piece is pulled down over the front of the sole with the lasting pincers and nailed down, using a welting or clogging hammer and blunt-ended round-headed nail. The upper is then secured at the sides, two nails each side, and the leather trimmed away with a knife. The steel toe-cap is inserted and hammered into position, above the inner leather toe-piece. The outer toe-piece is pulled down over the steel cap with the pincers and nailed down, with one nail at the front, and the leather trimmed with a knife. The welt, a narrow strip of leather, is now nailed down all the way round the sole, starting at the front and at roughly half-inch intervals. The nail-holes should be pierced at each place with the diamond awl, but it is as efficient without the pierced holes and time is also saved. The final step (in the case of the safety-clog) is to nail the metal toe-piece in position and hammer it into place—this is done to prevent the steel toe-cap in the safety clogs separating the leather from the wooden sole.

For specialised insulated clogs, rubber soles are attached to the soles. The craftsman is seated with the framework between his knees. This framework has been adapted for this particular use and the clog is placed on the wooden last. The rubber soles and heel pieces are simply nailed in place, using nails rather like screws. The overlapping rubber round the sole of the clog is trimmed off with the drag-knife and the inner part or straight edge of the heel trimmed with a paring knife. A 'pig's foot' is also used, to lift out nails not hammered in at the correct angle, or badly positioned nails; in this case the 'pig's foot' has a wooden handle, unlike the one used by the assemblers.

Boots

Although the rural bootmaker, once so common in all parts of Britain, is a rarity today, handmade boots and shoes are still in considerable demand. Bespoke boot and shoemakers are still found in most towns, while in the chief centres of the footwear trade in Leicestershire, Northamptonshire, Norfolk and Somerset, the hand bootmaker is still far from rare. He works in a trade where only fashion has changed, for the technique of boot-making has changed but little in hundreds of years. The hand bootmaker differs from his fellow worker in a large factory in that he is responsible for performing every operation from start to finish, while the factory worker is in the main responsible for only one process. It was only at a late stage that the bootmaking industry became highly mechanised, for hand work and simple tools tarried much longer in bootmaking than in almost any other trade. Woollen manufacturing, for example, was highly mechanised by the middle of the nineteenth century, but it was only during the first quarter of the present century that factory methods gradually supplanted traditional workmanship in the boot and shoe industry; indeed as hand craftsmen are still employed by large organisations, that process of mechanisation is far from complete.

The bootmaker requires a number of different qualities of leather for his craft. For example, shoe upper leather must be soft and supple, sheep skin or kid may be required for linings, while sole leather must be hard and durable. In addition, the quality of leather in the front or vamp of a shoe may be quite different from that used for the back or quarter of a shoe, while that used for the tongue may be different again. Cutting the various sections demands considerable knowledge of leather, for the parts have to be cut in such a way that there is very little wastage. A hide may vary considerably over its surface and the craftsman must know exactly what part to cut from a particular section of skin. Since boots are made in pairs, the bootmaker must pay attention not only to the colour of leather but also to its thickness and stretching qualities, so that each boot matches its fellow as nearly as possible in every respect.

The process of cutting the upper parts of a boot or shoe is known as 'clicking'. The equipment of the hand clicker is very simple, for all he requires is a cutting board and a knife. The cutting board is made up of small blocks of wood clamped together so that the knife edge cuts across the grain. In order to prevent the surface from becoming rough, this has to be scraped and smoothed at frequent intervals, for a rough surface hampers the free movement of the knife. The clicking knife is a short-bladed tool and although today clicking knives are fitted with blades that can be changed according to the type of leather that is to be cut, in the past the bootmaker required a series of knives. For example, to cut heavy, thick leather a curved blade was considered best, while for thin leather a straight-bladed clicking knife was necessary. In addition, the clicker requires an awl of small diameter, with a point some two and a half inches long, for making the guide holes for the assembly or closing operations. The cloth or kid linings of a boot must also be carefully cut to pattern by the clicker.

After clicking come the sequence of processes concerned with the preparation, fitting together and stitching the various sections to produce the completed uppers. These processes are known collectively as 'closing'. Some of the edges of the leather have to be reduced in thickness by paring away with a knife, so that seams may be produced without bulkiness. In some cases the leather has to be decorated with perforations while its edges may be serrated or gimped. The various sections are then stitched together with awl and thread. The craftsman usually makes his own thread from several straws of hemp twisted and waxed together and pointed with stout pig bristles at both ends. With the boot resting firmly between his knees and secured by a strap or piece of rope held firmly down with one foot, stitching begins. The awl pierces the leather, the bristles are inserted, crossed and pulled through to make a lockstitch. The stitches are flattened with a burnisher, irregularities are cut away and the boot upper is ready for lasting. Since the pattern of boots and shoes varies considerably, the process of closing also varies; ornamentation differs greatly, as does the pattern of stitching, the nature of the sections and the linings.

Perhaps the most complex of all the processes is that of bottoming; the shaping of insoles, heels, middle and outer soles. The outer sole and heels, since they receive most wear, are cut from butt leather, while the middle and insides are cut from the lighter portions of the hide; the bellies and shoulders in particular. First of all leather for soles is soaked in water in a narrow vessel. It is then hammered to solidify it and reduce its tendency to stretch. The insoles are tacked in place over a last, and when partially dry, two or three wooden pegs are driven in to hold it in place and the tacks removed. With a sharp knife, the leather is trimmed. The welt, which is the heavy leather to which the uppers are attached, is next sewn to the insole all around its edge, but before this is attached the edge has to be carefully flattened or thinned down. An awl with a bent point is used to perforate the insole at points where the welt is to be stitched. Heels are built up of layers or lifts of belly leather, finished with a single layer of butt leather. They are shaped with flat-headed hammer on a lap stone or lap iron; a smooth surface which is considered essential for the correct shaping and conditioning of sole leather. The middle and outer sole are treated in the same way, cut to shape and channelled with a line parallel to the outline of the sole. While the welt is sewn on with long stitches, averaging four to the inch, the sole is sewn on with very short stitches, possibly eight to the inch. The stitches are completed within the channel and they should have a regular pattern; considerable care is therefore necessary in piercing the sole with the awl.

After stitching the bottom is finished before the heel is put on. The stitch channel is closed by pressing it out towards the edge of the boot and rubbing it down to a smooth surface. The edges of the welt and sole are gently hammered until they are level and the bottom is rubbed with wet pumice stone. The heel is then fixed with wooden pegs and firmly stitched in place.

Finally the boot is lasted. The assembled uppers are strained with pliers over the metal or beechwood last which represents the shape of the customer's foot. The boot is then ready for sewing and the boot is polished and finished with great care. Lace-holes are cut, eyelets inserted and all irregularities smoothed down.

CHAPTER TEN

Chairs

The craft of chair-making is concentrated in the Wycombe district of Buckinghamshire and until recently in High Wycombe and the surrounding villages all the evolutionary stages in the craft, from the itinerant worker plying his trade in the solitude of the beech glades to the highly mechanised factories employing hundreds of specialists, could be seen. Villages such as Naphill, West Wycombe and Shockenchurch, possessed numerous small factories, employing no more than half a dozen specialized craftsmen; other villages had framing shops where the various parts of a chair made by other independent craftsmen were assembled. Although Buckinghamshire did have a number of independent craftsmen able to make a complete chair from beginning to the end, specialisation on certain parts of a chair has been a long characteristic of Wycombe craftsmen.

Undoubtedly the itinerant chair bodger, responsible for producing the turned parts of a chair, has been well known for many centuries, but the earliest mention of a chair-maker as such in a local record may be dated to 1793. The earliest workshops, which were small timber structures of two storeys, often in the backyard of a public house, were to be found in most Wycombe streets in the early nineteenth century. Many of the chair makers were innkeepers who employed benchmen and buttoners, framers and finishers, often paying them wages in kind. By 1835, when a survey of the town was carried out by the Parliamentary Commissioners, the manufacture of chairs had become well established and the industry in Wycombe employed two hundred men.

The principal craftsmen employed in chair making are the chair bodgers, responsible for the turned parts of a chair; benchmen who cut out splats, side rails, arms and other sawn parts; bottomers who adzed chair seats; benders responsible for boiling, bending and trimming bows for backs; framers who assembled chairs; finishers and polishers; and caners, often women out-workers, who made the rush cane or willow seats for certain types of chairs.

In some of the smaller factories, one craftsman would be responsible for more than one process, for example, benchmen often adzed chair seats, while framers were responsible for polishing as well as assembling. Nevertheless, the basic division of the labour force into benchmen and framers has continued to the present day. While benchmen are responsible for the rough shaping of chair parts, the framer is always responsible for assembling those parts and finishing them after they have come from the benchman's shop.

The bodger

Although fine Windsor chairs have been made of yew and cherry, the common Windsor was usually of beech with an ash bow and elm seat. Since prehistoric times the upper reaches of the Chilterns, with their cover of flinty clay overlying the chalk, have borne thick glades of beech. Here countless generations of chair bodgers have worked, drawing on the forests for their raw material. Beech is particularly well suited to the needs of the chair leg turner, for it cuts very smoothly while still green and it can also be cleft and left to dry for a considerable period without danger of warping or cracking. So profuse is the beech growth in the Chilterns that the tree is often called the 'Buckinghamshire weed' and it seems surprising that after hundreds, if not thousands, of bodgers have drawn on the wood over the years, the tree growth has remained as profuse as ever. This is in no small measure due to the techniques of felling adopted, a system that is known as 'the selection system'. When a bodger buys a stand of timber he does not proceed to cut it down indiscriminately, but selects those trees that will suit his purposes. The beech trunks he uses must not be too old, they must be straight-grained and have grown rather quickly. By the selection system the trees that are too small are left to grow, while any gaps in the forest will soon be filled by seedlings from the surrounding trees.

The tools and equipment required by the chair bodger are few and simple, and this, together with the fact that there is a great deal of wastage of raw material, explains why chair leg making throughout the centuries always remained a woodland craft. In a trade where more elaborate tools are required, and where there is little wastage of timber, underwood industries have tended to become localised in village workshops. It is so very much easier for the craftsman to take his simple equipment to the woodlands than it is to have timber, often from inaccessible places, taken to a permanent workshop.

After buying a stand of timber from one of the Chiltern land-owners, the bodger moves into the beech glade and sets up his portable shelter. Although in recent times bodgers used prefabricated wooden or corrugated iron sheds, the traditional hut was built up of wood shavings. An elderly bodger interviewed in 1955 said:

> The straight saplings were chosen, cut in twelve foot lengths and split down the middle. The top was joined by boring a hole through each some ten inches from the tip through which a tapered peg was inserted and tapped tight. These formed the two ends and were braced three feet from the ground. These frames were erected at suitable distances to allow for the lathe and pole and shaving horse. Across the top and resting in the forks a cross-bar was placed. Side rails were nailed on and the whole framework was covered with four thatched bundles to within four feet of the ground. After work had been in progress and enough waste about, the walls were built . . . these huts were beautifully warm for the thick wall of shavings kept out all draughts.

The whole process of establishing a workshop in a new stand of timber could easily be completed in a day.

After felling the beech trunks are trimmed with an axe, the branches lopped off and the trunks cut into eighteen inch billets with a crosscut saw. This has unraked and widely set teeth and is designed to cut both ways. On a visit to a bodger in Hampden woods in 1958 it was found that the craftsman worked alone, but he was still able to use this particular type of saw though it was designed for operation by two people. The one isolated incident of a man using a tool designed for two epitomises the great change that has taken place in rural Britain. Each trunk is rolled into position on a pair of home-made sawing dogs for cutting up, and after sawing the billets are cleft with a beetle and short handled wedge, on a low chopping block, the aim of this operation being to reduce the log to sizes that will give pieces for chair legs, with as little wastage as possible. Some billets may yield only four pieces, others may yield as many as sixteen. The homemade beetle is a short-handled tool ringed to prevent splitting, while the wedge is more in the nature of a splitting out hatchet with a blade no more than three inches wide.

The cleft pieces are next trimmed to a roughly octagonal shape, the billets resting on a high chopping block and cut with a small side-axe. This tool with a blade sharpened on one side only, has a handle six inches long, and with a few deft strokes the craftsman reduces the block of wood to the rough outline of a chair leg.

Placing the roughly shaped leg in the jaws of a shaving horse, the wood is shaved with a draw knife. The shaving horse is a low bench which many woodland craftsmen use for shaping timber. The craftsman sits astride the horse, pressing down the foot lever, so as to hold the piece of wood under the clamp. The bodger's horse differs from that used by other wood workers in that pieces of serrated steel are inserted in the clamping blocks. These are necessary to prevent the green beech from suddenly slipping into the workman's chest. The draw knife, which in the past was widely used by most woodland craftsmen, consists of a narrow blade basilled on its upper side with two handles fitted to it at right angles. It is pulled with both hands to shave chair legs to very nearly the correct shape and proportion of the finished product.

The final, and perhaps the most complicated, stage in chair bodging is the turning of the leg on the lathe. The bodger was the last of the woodland craftsmen to use a type of lathe that has been in use since the Iron Age—the pole lathe. Two beams of wood are fixed horizontally on legs to form the bed of the lathe. They are parallel to each other, but a few inches apart, so that there is a groove between them. This groove receives the tenons of the puppets which are wedged to it. The puppets can be moved according to the size of material to be worked by removing the wedges. A fixed five-eights-inch screw is fitted to one puppet as a centre, while the other centre is adjustable. The chair bodger's pole lathe differs from those of other woodworkers, for example that used by Bucklebury bowl turners, in that the driving string is wrapped directly around the material to be turned and the lathe is not equipped with a chuck. The driving power is a twelve foot ash or larch pole, firmly fixed to the ground and supported by the sides of the hut in the centre. A piece of string joins the end of the pole to the foot treadle, being wrapped once or twice around the material first. By pressing the foot treadle, which is hinged to the back of the hut, the pole bends and the material turns the spring back again when the foot is removed. The great disadvantage of the pole lathe is the fact that the chisel can only be applied on the forward movement of the material and the down stroke of the foot.

In turning a chair leg one end is tapped on to the fixed centre and the cord passed around it twice. The other end is centred by turning the screwed shank of the adjustable centre. The wood is adjusted for true running and a small half-inch gouge is used to rough the surface. Traditional Windsor chairs have bobbin decorations on the legs, and are cut with V-shaped chisels. The turning process from start to finish takes no more than two minutes.

All this work is carried out while the wood is still green and the finished chair legs are stacked to dry for weeks before being transported to the Wycombe factories.

The benchman

The benchman is responsible for cutting the sawn parts of the chair, using beech for the legs, stretchers, banisters and many other parts, yew for bow and elm for the chair seat. The timber he requires is delivered in the form of planks to his workshop and in the past these were cut by specialised pit sawyers, well known in the Buckinghamshire woodlands. The benchman's traditional tool is the bow or frame saw known in the Wycombe district as a 'Betty', 'Dancing Betty' or 'Jesus Christ' saw.[1] These vary in size from a large 'Up and Down' saw, with a blade some thirty inches long for sawing the larger parts, to a small bow saw with a blade no more than seven inches long for cutting out the intricate pattern of a wheelback Windsor. The latter process is long and laborious, 'for every piercing—and some banisters had as many as twenty—meant boring a hole, dismantling a bow saw, threading the blade through the hole, reassembling the bow saw, cutting out the piece, dismantling the bow saw, and so on until the whole pattern had been completed'.[2]

The bow saw itself is a tool of great antiquity with a blade strained along the margin of a frame tightened by means of a rope at the other side. Its great advantage lies in the fact that the blade can be adjusted to any angle. For the benchman's work of cutting out a great variety of shapes and sizes, the frame saw is therefore far superior to the open hand saw used by most other woodworkers. A great deal of material for a chair has to be sawn at a cant while the intricate patterns of banisters and splats can only be cut with highly adjustable tools.

The bottomer

While the benchman's characteristic tool is the bow saw, the bottomer's essential is a long-handled, razor-sharp, hollowing adze. This has a curved wooden handle some 28 inches long and a blade some 3 inches wide and 9 inches long. The blank elm seats, each some 18 inches square and 2 inches thick, are sawn to shape by the benchman with a large up and down bow saw, but the bottomer is responsible for their shaping. In the past the bottomer was a specialised, highly skilled workman, who undertook no work but the adzing of chair seats. The smoothing of the seats was left to the framer who, with his spokeshaves and scrapers, reduced the bottomer's work to a smooth finish. H. E. Goodchild, a notable maker of Windsor chairs at Naphill, was the son of a specialised bottomer.

Today, modern routing machines are able to complete bottoming very quickly, and the ancient adze has become obsolete in an industry where it was once such a vital tool. The method of using the adze is for the bottomer to place the seat blank on the floor, holding it firmly in place with both feet. The blank is then quickly reduced to the correct shape with a quick chopping motion of the adze, at right-angles to the run of the grain. In some cases the seat blank is held in position for working by being mounted on a base—an unwanted or faulty seat with four screws projecting and piercing the underside of the seat. After the adzing is complete, the seat is a maze of irregular ridges and hollows. At one place it is perhaps two inches deep, at others it is no more than half an inch, and before completion, these ridges and hollows have to be smoothed with spokeshaves and scrapers, the framer's task.

The bender

The chair back is framed with a bow of which both ends are fixed in the seat. The best bows are made of cleft yew or ash stakes, roughly squared with the draw knife before bending, but most chairs are equipped with bows sawn out of a plank. After trimming each bow has to be steamed or boiled until pliable and bent on a bending table. This consists of a low table with a block of wood and wooden pegs screwed to its surface. The bow is wedged to the correct position, the loose ends bound with twine. When dry and set to the correct shape, the bow is removed from the table, a strut is fitted to maintain its position and is then sent to the framing shop.

The framer

One of the most skilled of all workmen in the furniture industry is the framer; the craftsman responsible for finishing and assembling chairs. It is his duty, not only to smooth the legs, seats and other parts that come to him in a rough condition from bodgers, benchmen, bottomers and benders, but he has to bore dozens of mortice holes in bows, legs, stretchers, and seats. He has to tenon the various parts and glue and wedge the whole chair together. If the chair is not to be sold 'in the white' or passed on to a specialised polisher, it is his duty to stain it as well. Unlike the other craftsmen in the trade, who use but one or two tools, the framer possesses an extensive tool-kit of equipment rarely seen in any other trade. His characteristic piece of equipment is the breast bib, a wooden bar measuring 10 by 3 inches, supported by leather harness, designed to protect the framer's chest when boring mortice holes. A recess in the centre of the bar is designed to accommodate the rotating heads of the wooden braces and the long-shanked screwdriver that the craftsman constantly uses. Boring is a highly skilled process for the various rails and stretchers enter the other members at different angles. For example, the back rails of a chair enter the seat and the bow at different angles, while the back legs of a chair must slope out at the back. All the boring is done by eyesight and considerable craftsmanship is required, for the framer uses no pattern or written calculations to help him in his work.

The framing block on which the boring is done is nothing more than a low, heavy bench on which the work is secured by wedging it between three protruding pegs. Traditionally the beech-stocked braces that the farmer uses have permanently fixed spoon bits and each one is known by the type of work it is designed for. Thus a framer will have a 'legging bit', 'a stump bit', 'a bow bit' and 'a stick bit', each one being from a quarter to one inch wide. Every framing shop has a large number of these. To sharpen the bits a scraping tool, made of an old triangular file is used, while the final sharpening has to be done with an oil stone slip.

19 H. E. Goodchild of Naphill, Bucks. making a chair leg

20 Chair legs produced by a bodger in Hampden woods, Bucks.

21 Carpenters at work on part of a ship

The framer never uses a plane for smoothing, for all parts of the chair are smoothed with a series of spokeshaves. Some like the 'travisher' have convex blades, others like the 'devil' have straight blades, while the 'smoker back hollow knife' has a concave blade. The final finish is obtained with scrapers often ground down from pieces of old, broken saw blades. Each scraper is first of all sharpened with an oil stone and then turned in the manner of a currier's knife with a 'ticketer'—an old cobbler's awl. Scratch tools, somewhat similar to the scrapers, are used to produce the shallow mouldings found on some chairs. In addition the framer uses a number of two-handled draw knives, morticing and firmer chisels, gouges, a steel-faced framing hammer, calipers for setting out, screwdriver and reamers. A stove is essential for drying out wedges and tenons as well as for drying out the various parts of the chair, for the parts cannot be assembled until they are bone dry and fully seasoned.

Finally with wedges and glue the chair is assembled and although some are sold 'in the white', others are taken to the staining or polishing shop.

The finisher and stainer

Today, finishing and polishing is a mechanical process and the craftsman uses spray guns and other pieces of modern equipment to complete the work very quickly. In the past, however, hand staining and polishing was a lengthy process and for the more expensive chairs it demanded considerable skill and craftsmanship.

Chairs were first of all cleaned down with nitric acid, an undesirable task, usually performed by young boys. Each chair was then immersed in a heated tank containing a solution of wood chips and water until it was completely stained. A variety of combs were then used to add grain decoration.

Some of the cheaper chairs were polished by oiling with linseed oil, 'some were waxed, some had a coat or two of shellac polish slapped on with a brush, while the best work had the full french polish treatment or was highly polished and then dulled to a satin finish with pumice powder or similar abrasives'.[3] The polisher's equipment consisted of no more than a quantity of rag and wadding, half a dozen grades of sandpaper and a length of horsehair rope used for rubbing down the more inaccessible parts of the chair. The craftsman always worked at a low bench in a well-heated workshop and in most cases the craftsman in question, like others in the chair making industry, was a specialist who undertook staining and polishing for a large number of framers.

The caner

Although a large proportion of the chairs made by Buckinghamshire craftsmen in the past were all wooden, cane or rush bottomed chairs were equally well known. By tradition, the actual caning was carried out by women, who were often out-workers carrying on the trade at piece-work rates in their own homes. The actual preparation of the cane, however, was man's work, and the 'marker-off', as he was known, split canes with a knife blade and wedge and finished them on a marking-off board. This consisted of nothing more than a plank some 15 inches long and 5 inches wide with sets of razor-sharp blades piercing its surface in V-shaped pairs. The distance between each blade could be regulated by turning a screw to contain the width of cane required. In addition, each marking-off board had a horizontal blade, so that the pith could be removed by pulling the cane beneath it.

The actual caning, a simple process though a great variety of patterns was evolved, was carried out by women and children with the minimum of equipment. This consisted of nothing more than an old knife for cane cutting, a small mallet to drive in the wooden pegs used to attach the cane, and a few awl-like pegs for clearing holes.

Rush matting was also used for seat bottoms, but the actual sorting and plaiting of rushes was hard and dirty work, demanding some skill. The inside of the seat had to be stuffed with broken rushes, but before these could be used they had to be soaked in water to make them pliable. The women carried out their tasks on a workshop floor and the work was considered so unhealthy that Wycombe matters had to have a monthly medical examination. The matter's tool kit was again simple—an iron peg, a wooden rubber, a knife and a stuffing stick.

CHAPTER ELEVEN

Cutlery and Edge Tools

The hand-forging of cutlery is a craft industry that has declined alarmingly within the last few years, mainly due to the mechanisation of forging processes and the consequent standardisation of cutlery design. In the highly skilled spring blade section of the industry, there were about three hundred cutlers in Sheffield no more than forty years ago; by 1969 this small branch of the industry was represented by no more than three elderly practitioners. Hand-forging has been replaced in every branch of the cutlery industry by mechanical processes. Maching forging or 'goffing' has almost entirely replaced the skill and craftsmanship of the hand-forger; blades are placed between rollers and shapes cut out by machine. Even the hardening and tempering processes, representing the greatest skills of the hand-forger, have given way to heat treatment in furnaces where temperature is strictly controlled automatically, with the quenching and tempering processes being automated under pyrometric control.

The hand-forging of blades demanded considerable skill and an eight-year apprenticeship was necessary to achieve full competence. 'A boy who starts learning the trade at thirteen years of age', says one writer, 'should be able at the age of eighteen to forge through the pen blade or pocket blade. He has to learn to mood or mould first, then the tanging process, and afterwards smithing or finishing the blade. . . . By the time he is twenty-one all the processes should have been mastered for the simplest type of blade.'[1]

The Sheffield cutlery industry was never highly organised, for though the large factories employed many cutlers, the majority of the craftsmen were independent master craftsmen, who worked on their own account in a large number of back street workshops. After serving apprenticeships, these 'little mesters' as they were called, set up business on their own account, and the 'little mesters' more than anyone contributed to the worldwide reputation of Sheffield as a centre of the cutlery industry. Most of the craftsmen specialised in a particular branch of the cutlery trade; some were specialists in pruning knives or scissors or pen blades, others in table knives, razors or forks. The spring knife and scissors sections of the industry were by tradition singlehanded trades, where one man working on his own was responsible for all the processes. In making table knives, razors and forks however, the processes were always doublehanded, with the master cutler requiring the assistance of a striker, who was also usually responsible for the hardening processes. In this way, while the smith forged, the striker could see to the hardening process, for in the cutlery trade speed was all-important, and the hand-forger depended for his livelihood on the speed at which he worked.

This was one reason why each forger specialised in a particular branch of the cutlery industry, for by specialising, there was no need to change the tools and patterns used for making a particular knife. Practice and familiarity too led to efficiency and speed and it has been estimated that in the spring knife section of the industry, a good workman could expect to turn out approximately ten dozen pairs during the course of a full working day. 'In the 1880s', says one recent writer 'the average skilled craftsman was receiving a weekly wage of between thirty and thirty five shillings. However, even after the turn of the century, there were many branches of the trade in which wages could be as low as only half this amount.'[2] The working day often lasted from 8.15 a.m. to 7.45 p.m., 'with twenty minutes off for dinner and ten minutes off for tea'. An elderly forger, speaking of his old master, calculated that he forged 'one gross of pairs during a working day . . . and for this he earned seven shillings and sixpence'. Even from this low gross wage, deductions were made for gas lighting and even for toilet facilities.

During the early years of the present century, conditions were not much better, for every hand-forger worked on a piece rate basis; the average rate for pen blades being approximately four shillings per gross of 168. The normal working week was usually sixty-two hours distributed as follows: Monday—8 a.m. to 6 p.m.; Tuesday—8 a.m. to 7 p.m.; Wednesday, Thursday and Friday—8 a.m. to 8 p.m. and Saturday 8 a.m. to 1 p.m. The Sheffield master cutler, often working singlehanded, was responsible for ordering work from his counterparts in the forging and grinding sections, hawking the completed wares around the country and then paying the forger and grinder out of his profits after the whole deal had been completed. Hand-forgers often undertook work for larger firms and received payment on a piece rate from cutlery merchants when their own particular part of the process was completed.

According to Abel Bywater in his *Sheffield Dialect* of 1839 there were four distinct steps concerning 'iverra thing ats dun to a pen knife throot furst to last'. '1st he moodst blade', Bywater says, '2nd he tangs it, 3rd he smithies it and 4th he hardens an tempers it and then he's done we't.' All this work is done with a variety of tools and equipment in a workshop and around the hearth, which is the centre of the forge. This hearth is either of iron or of brick and is usually considerably smaller than an ordinary village blacksmith's forge. It usually stands about 30 inches high, the actual height depending largely on the individual craftsman's preferences. Usually along the front of the hearth and extending its whole width, is found an iron plate of considerable thickness, firmly embedded in the masonry. This measures approximately 25 inches long and 9 inches deep, and on it the blade is tapped as soon as it is removed from the fire to dislodge any pieces of coke or scale that may still adhere to the surface of the steel. Near this hearth plate too is a trough of water used for quenching the hot metal in the final tempering process.

The traditional fuel used by hand-forgers was charcoal and until quite recently many preferred charcoal to any other fuel for high quality steel blades. By 1939, however, charcoal had become very scarce and hand-forgers searched for other fuels. The fuel preferred was gas coke, each piece of coke being about the size of a garden pea. Many too used coal slack, but this was far from satisfactory. Coke is still used, but since the forgers have met considerable difficulty in obtaining the correct size of coke, it is customary to cut up large pieces to obtain the correct dimensions. The hearth fire, lit every morning, is small and concentrated and may not measure more than a few inches across. A great deal of the skill of the hand forger is shown in his ability to build a fire; knowing exactly how to place the fuel in order to get the maximum intensity of heat, and knowing exactly where he has to hold the metal before forging. One of the difficulties in a forger's shop is the high sulphur content of the fumes that emanate from the hearth, so that a characteristic of all forges is the large tapering cowl of metal or brick, designed to carry away the smoke and fumes.

Oddly enough, electrically driven fans and bellows that find favour in most blacksmith's shops have never been greatly favoured by the hand-forgers of Sheffield. Bellows of the traditional pear shape or the more modern hand-operated round type have persisted, mainly due to the fact that they provide a more controllable draught. This saves a great deal of overheating and the consequent wastage of steel. In both types of bellows, an air blast is produced by both the upward and downward swings of the bellows arm or foot treadle, so that the draught is continuous rather than intermittent.

In forging a knife blade, the craftsman must be very careful in the choice of steel, ensuring that the right type of steel is chosen for a particular piece of cutlery and ensuring that it has the right combination of characteristics for a particular purpose. For such things as butchers' cleavers or carving knives, which must stand up to regular and constant sharpening, the best quality sheet steel is required; for razors, the best quality razor steel, which has to take the keenest edge possible, which must possess uniformity of temper and be capable of a high polish is necessary. Consequently, in the past, razor steel only containing 0.75 per cent carbon was used, while today carbon content is no higher than 1·25 per cent. According to elderly cutlers, high carbon steel is much more difficult to work than that containing a low proportion of carbon. In the cutlery industry, ease of working is one of the craftsman's main considerations.

In a forger's workshop, one of the most essential pieces of equipment is the 'stiddy' or anvil, placed below a well lighted window. In describing an anvil in a Sheffield forger's workshop, Atkin gives details regarding the manufacture of anvils in the city. 'The hand forger's anvil', he says, 'weighs from three to four hundredweights and has a hardened steel face, three gates, three haggon holes, two becks, the one on the right with a horn or pointed beck, and four or five nail mark holes. The main body of the anvil is known as the butt and is made from iron, usually obtained by melting down horse shoes because of their purity. The dimensions of the butt are approximately: depth 16 inches; length 18 inches; width 6 inches. Each of the gates is approximately $1\frac{1}{2}$ inches wide, and the haggon holes and nail mark holes are about 1 inch by $\frac{1}{2}$ inch. The face is a six inch square plate of 3 inch thick hardened steel, hammer welded to the butt. Tom Merrill' [a cutler studied by Atkin in detail] 'uses a Mousehole anvil, i.e. one made by the forge of that name in Hillsborough (a suburb of Sheffield). This firm, like all the others that used to make anvils in Sheffield, is now out of business. Tom tells me it is always possible to pick out a Mousehole anvil from those made by either Binney or Taylor (the two other main manufacturers) because the Mousehole anvil is always soft-faced. This means that the centre of the face is soft and tends to mark easily, and sometimes even to lift after much use. The edges, on the other hand, are brittle and tend to break or flake off. Taylor and Binney Anvils do not have this drawback.

'The secret of this difference lies in the hardening process used. At the Mousehole forge, when the butt was to be faced with steel, both the butt and the face would be raised to welding heat in separate fires because the two metals were required to be at different temperatures. Then, when the blacksmith shouted "Reet" the two would be brought together and the face put into position. Four strikers would then hammer them into a weld, working from the centre out so as to expel all the air (any air pockets would cause the face to lift at a later date) and also to make sure that the centre was the firmest part of the weld. Finally, the gates would be opened out by driving a wedge shaped stake down them, and the whole would be left to cool. After a couple of days, the anvil would be reheated, but to less than a welding temperature, and afterwards placed in a trough of water to a depth of about two inches below the weld. Binney served his apprenticeship at the Mousehole forge but was quick to realise that the above method of cooling, or sizzling as it was known, caused incorrect hardening of the steel face. The edges cooled first and were therefore left hardest. Binney pointed this out, but his ideas were not accepted at the Mousehole forge so he struck out on his own. At his forge, when the time came for the cooling and hardening of the face, four fire hoses played on the centre of the face and gradually moved outwards to the corners so that the middle was left hard and the edges softer. Taylor was the son-in-law of Binney and used exactly the same process as he did. Anvil-making of this type is one of the lost arts; nowhere in England today is it possible to have a face welded to the butt by the blacksmith in the old manner. Acetylene welding has been tried but it has not met with the approval of the old hand-forgers. The hand forger's anvil has to be carefully set in a block of stone, but it is important that the metal of the anvil does not actually touch the stone base. Bedding was therefore a most important process, and horse manure to a depth of two inches or more was laid in the hole on the anvil base and the anvil was allowed to settle on this. Four wedges were then driven in to keep it in position. Springiness and perfect vibrations are important considerations in anvils and it is said that once set, a good bedding of horse manure should last the whole life of an anvil.'

The forger uses a variety of punches; some of them reverse punches that are used to impart the reverse of their own shapes to metal blanks. The punches, like most of the hand forger's equipment, are made by the craftsman himself from cast steel, with working faces carefully tempered and hardened to withstand constant hammering. Many of the tools are like the blacksmith's bottom swages and fullers, designed for fitting into tool holes in the cavity surface. Each tool has its position on the anvil: 'The back boss is situated at the back of the anvil in the first gate, that is the one nearest the face. It is shaped with an angle that drops away from the forger and it is used for drawing out the steel bar during the mooding process.' For tanging, smithing and straightening the blade, a flat boss, fitted in an orifice in front of the first, is used. In front of this is a round boss with a curved surface on which the blade is flattened by constant hammering and the shoulders shaped. The cutting off haggar for cutting the blade off occupies a tool hole at the back of the anvil, while a tanging haggar is also required. For testing the resistance and strength of a blade the craftsman used a so-called devil, an iron stake some 6 inches long with a U-shaped slot cut into its top face. This again fits into an orifice in the anvil's surface.

Hand forgers used two pear-shaped hammers; the first weighing between 4 and 6 pounds for the initial shaping of 'mooding' of the blade; the second weighing no more than 2 pounds for the process of tanging and smithing. The face of the hammer is not set at right-angles to the sides, but in fact inclines from front to back. The reason for this is that the hammer must strike the work squarely, and the slope of the face when combined with the angle of the arm at the bottom of the stroke does actually produce this effect. The hammer is either made from steel throughout or, like the anvil, from iron faced with steel on the main working surface. Taylor, the anvil maker, was the main producer of this steel-faced iron hammer, while Vardey's of Eldon Street were the first people to produce the all-steel type. Whichever variety is used, the steel working surface has to be specially hardened to withstand the constant hard work. So too, the face has to be ground periodically to keep it smooth and of the correct shape.

The average pen or pocket blade takes approximately ninety-five hammer blows to fashion; consequently, it will be seen that each hammer must be perfectly balanced if undue strain on the forger's arm is to be avoided. He may be forging as many as one gross of pairs (matching pen and pocket blades) during the course of a single working day. As a cutler's dozen consists of fourteen blades, not the customary twelve, this would mean 336 blades or 66,800 strokes of a hammer which would weigh an average of some 28 pounds. There is obviously no room here for any wasted effort.

This can be seen from the fact that when a forger has finished using his hammer he does not waste energy in stopping it dead. He allows it to bounce up and down two or three times on the anvil face until it comes to rest naturally. The process also illustrates the forger's concern with 'spring' and the correct 'vibrations' in his tools. A skilled craftsman can tell exactly what article another is forging and what point in the process of manufacture has been reached merely by listening to the ring of the anvil. Indeed, in the old days, when there were a lot of hand-forgers working together, to those who could appreciate it, it was like listening to a great orchestra. Every worker's stroke could be picked out amid the clang and ring of the anvils. The various rhythms were so regular that one helped the other to get on with his work. Now these are becoming extinct. Nearly all the hand-forgers have ceased to operate. In addition, the hand-forger requires a variety of tongs and fine bits, most of these of his own manufacture.

The most highly skilled stage of the cutler's craftsmanship is the final tempering of steel blades, for which mooding, tanging and smithing are largely mechanical processes, demanding strength and dexterity, that of the final heat treatment of blades being judged by the forger solely on the basis of experience. Tempering begins with the process of annealing, when the bullets of forged steel are softened by heating them to a clear red heat and allowing them to cool naturally. The steel blades are then hardened by dipping the reheated steel to a red heat, and quenching it in the water trough at the side of the hearth. It is left in the water for about five seconds, withdrawn and allowed to 'blue'. After a few minutes cooling it is again plunged into water and left there until cold. This process is known as 'slacking the blade'. Oil is occasionally used as a substitute for water when a less intense effect is desired. The final process is that of hardening, when the blade is heated again and allowed to cool gradually. Finally the blade was cleaned and ground.

Until 1920 the 'cutler's dozen' of fourteen and a gross of 168 was the usual measurement of quantity used in the cutlery trade, and it was only through the efforts of the unions that the regular twelve to a dozen was adopted in Sheffield. One of the most interesting facets of the Sheffield cutlery industry is that of making scythe and sickle blades, a craft industry that has declined considerably due to low demand within recent years. When the Sheffield Cutler's Company was incorporated in 1624, thirty-one members were described as makers of sickles and shears, but gradually the craft of making agricultural tools became separate from the true cutlery industry, and in addition to its location in the Sheffield district, the Midlands of England were equally important centres of manufacture. In scythe-making, for example, riveted back scythes, where blades made from sheet steel, strengthened along the backs into bars of tougher metal were chiefly made in Sheffield, but crown scythes made from bars of metal welded and forged together were made exclusively in Belbroughton and several adjoining villages in Worcestershire.

The restored Abbeydale scythe-forging works at Sheffield provides an example of a fully comprehensive works where the product was riveted back scythes. In making this type of tool high calibre steel is required and this is cut into a blank which is made wider at the top in order to allow for a flange to be turned over. The bar at the back of the scythe is fitted and the flange has to be made with considerable care. After punching the scythe blade for the rivet holes and grass holes, the groove or 'grist' into which the back bar fits is stamped out. The blades, in batches of half a dozen or so, are hardened by placing in a furnace; they are then plunged in an oil bath. The blades are then placed in a small furnace for tempering, with only the back of each subjected to full heat. As the heat increases, the metal changes colour and is removed from the heat at the crucial moment. The scythe-back consists of a piece of oblong metal, heated and beaten out on the tilt hammer and finished by hand on the anvil. Accuracy is absolutely essential in this process, and the back is riveted on to the tempered blade, before the whole tool is ground on a large water-driven wheel.

Crown scythes with blades up to 60 inches long were also made at the Abbeydale Works, but the real home of this type of scythe was the villages of Worcestershire, with Belbroughton as its centre. The crown scythe consists of four bars of metal—a bar of blister steel, two bars of pure charcoal iron and a bar of mild steel at the back. The weight of the mild steel bar should be equal to the weight of the other three bars. The four bars are forged together under the heavy blows of a tilt hammer. After forging, the combination of bars produced a strong spine of mild steel with a fine cutting edge supported by sides of iron. Gripping the bars of metal with tongs, the metal is heated until hot enough to forge, by repeated hammer blows from the tilt hammer. From one series of metal bars, two blades are made, for after forging one end of the bars they are turned around, the other end forged in the same way and the fully forged bars cut into two with large shears. After plating, tempering, grinding and polishing, the scythe blade is more or less complete. This was basically the method of making all agricultural edge tools from turnip hakes to fagging hooks.

Grinding was a process that demanded considerable knowledge and dexterity and in describing a grinding shop in Belbroughton, Hennell says:

> The grinding house consists of a float with deep trenches on either side; the grind stones, which are four feet or more in diameter and nine inches across, revolved away from the grinders, who are mounted astride wooden horses so that they can press the blade with both hands on the whizzing stone. A jet of water plays on the stone and is carried away by the trench, but notwithstanding the water the blade throws out sparks like a firework. The noise is immense, making speech useless; there is a high singing note which except for its loudness would be musical. Great improvements have been made on behalf of the workers, who were formerly liable to silicosis, a disease caused by inhaling particles of the local ferrous sandstone, which was traditionally used. . . . Sandstone grinding is still to be seen and heard in the Sheffield district, a rougher, interrupted neighing sound. Here the stones spin towards the grinder, but in Worcestershire away from him.'[3]

CHAPTER TWELVE

Needles

The Redditch district of Worcestershire has long been regarded as the centre of the needle-making industry, but it was not until the early years of the nineteenth century that the town became the true centre of the industry. 'Not more than forty years since', says a writer in 1854, 'Redditch was only a third rate needle-making village and in 1799 a greater number were made by one firm in Studley than were produced by all the needle makers of Redditch.'[1] Nearby Studley together with Alcester in Warwickshire were earlier centres of needle-making, and during the eighteenth century these two Warwickshire towns were far more important than Redditch for needle-manufacturing, while in earlier centuries Long Crendon in Buckinghamshire and Whitechapel in London were the most important needle-producers. In London, for example, the Guild of Needlemakers was incorporated in 1656, and the needlemakers earned for themselves such a reputation that in the eighteenth century 'Alcester needle makers, jealous of the fame of the London needles, labelled their common qualities with Whitechapel labels; by this means and the greater facilities for making needles in Warwickshire, needles soon ceased to be made in London'.[2] Long Crendon in Buckinghamshire had also been a centre of needle-manufacturing since the mid-sixteenth century, and throughout the seventeenth century and the greater part of the eighteenth, needle-making, particularly the making of large sail and packing needles, was regarded as the town's staple industry. Gradually the needle-making industry at Long Crendon declined in importance in the late eighteenth century, mainly because the needle-makers 'looked with contempt on what they called new-fangled ways of making needles and continued to make them in the good old ways'.[3]

Although the making of sail needles continued to be practised at Long Crendon until the second half of the nineteenth century many

Buckinghamshire craftsmen migrated to the Studley and Alcester districts of Warwickshire during the first decade of the nineteenth century. This steady migration to the Midlands continued until the 1860s, by which time Redditch reigned supreme as the principal needle-manufacturing town of Britain. As a correspondent in the *Illustrated London News* in 1851 wrote: 'Needles may have been made in London and Long Crendon formerly, but at the present time no needles worth mention are made in any city, town, village or place excepting Redditch.' Undoubtedly it was during the first half of the nineteenth century that Redditch attained pre-eminence as the centre of the industry, for an observer in 1799 wrote that 'in this hamlet of Redditch there is a considerable manufacture of needles; about 400 persons are employed here and in the neighbourhood about 2000'[4] but Alcester and Studley across the county boundary in Warwickshire were regarded as l ˙ng more important centres of manufacture.

There are no obvious reasons to suggest why Redditch became the centre of needle-manufacture and the reasons for the location of the industry are purely fortuitous. Water power from the rivers Arrow and Alne, a plentiful supply of coal and proximity to wire works may have all contributed to the growth of the industry in Worcestershire and Warwickshire. By 1850 there was 'scarcely a village within ten miles of Redditch' that did not 'contribute its share of these useful articles'.

Until about 1830 needle-making was principally a hand process and certain parts of the manufacturing process were carried out by outworkers in their own homes. Traditionally, there is division of labour in this craft industry and no one person was ever responsible for the whole manufacturing process. 'Needle making was a trade', says Diderot, simple in principle but studied in practice, which might be taken as an illustration that both division of labour and a consequent monotony of routine were characteristic of certain branches of manufacture long before the Industrial Revolution.'[5]

The first sequence of processes in needle-making are concerned with preparing the wire and this was a process undertaken by wire-drawers rather than by the needle-makers themselves. In the early nineteenth century German, but especially Hungarian steel, was greatly preferred in the industry. 'Heat it under pit of charcoal', says an eighteenth century writer:

Lay it red hot under the hammer to take away its angles, to lengthen it out and round it. Have ready a wire drawing iron with different holes; draw your steel wire through one of the larger holes to make it finer; then having reheated it, through a smaller hole. . . . Continue in this manner till your wire is reduced by those successive drawings to the degree of fineness which is required for the needles you intend to make.[6]

THE EYEING PRESS.

Fig. 6 Making needle eyes on the press

By the end of the nineteenth century, little wire-drawing was practised in the Redditch district but wire was brought to the area in bundles from works in Sheffield and elsewhere.

Until the end of the first quarter of the nineteenth century, the processes of needle-making were principally carried out by hand, in small workshops and in the homes of needle-makers. It was a craft industry widely distributed throughout the Studley–Alcester–Redditch area, in village cottages as well as town workshops. The wire was cut by means of a guillotine into the correct needle lengths. The craftsman stood alongside the bench that carried the guillotine, and with a bunch of wires in his left hand he pressed the handle of the guillotine so that the lengths of wire fell into a receptacle at the front of the bench. The lengths of wire were then passed to a second workman, who after heating the wires flattened the heads, four at a time, ready to receive the eyes. The wires were then placed on a small lead blank and the steel punched out, in two stages. First a punch with a sharp, short point was used to mark the eye, and this was followed by the second punch, which had a long fine point. A small pair of pliers, called 'torp', was required, with a shallow groove to hold the needle, and a groove or gutter was formed on each side of the eye with a saw-edged file called a 'guttering-iron'. Finally the head was trimmed off with a file. Foot-worked stamping machines for shaping the eyes of the needles 'in double length, two needles head to head were first introduced into the trade about 1825. They rapidly replaced the old "soft-work" process so that by 1830 most of the soft-workers were thrown out of employment. There was a strike and serious rioting, the stamps in use being smashed.'[7]

The pointing of needles in the early nineteenth century was more often than not performed by outworkers, although a water-driven mill was used for needle-pointing as early as 1700 at Studley. Hand-pointing persisted until well into the nineteenth century.

It was a deadly occupation, for in spite of the fact that the workers at this process wore cloth mufflers over mouth and nose, the fine metallic and mineral dust found its way into the respiratory passages and organs, causing inflammation of the nostrils and larynx and atrophy of the lungs. . . . The effects of pointing were early visible on the workmen and with hard drinking, hard fighting and when so-disposed hard working, their constitution soon began to give way.

Attempts were made in the early nineteenth century to lessen the harmful effects of metal dust, first by magnets and then by fans which 'lessened the disease and mortality rate among the pointers . . . but its compulsory use was warmly resented by the pointers who regarded it as an attempt to lower the importance and money value of their work. . . . Still more hotly did they resent and oppose the use of the pointing machine, the introduction of which about 1875 led to serious disturbances.'[8]

> It is horrible to think [said Morrall] that any portion of our fellow creatures should be subject to such an ordeal, but from the high rate of remuneration offered, and the fact that there are many, who from loss of character are not enabled to obtain employment at other branches of the business, no difficulty has hitherto been found in obtaining a sufficient number of operatives to perform the work.[9]

The methods of pointing adopted under the old pre-factory system of manufacture, were that the needle pointer, seated in front of a grindstone, took a bunch of needles

> spread them out so that they lay singly, but close together with their ends perfectly even, and then introduces them between the

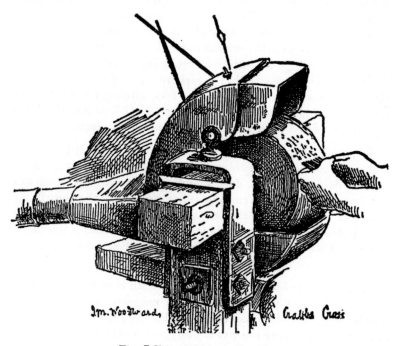

Fig. 7 Sharpening needle points

24 Oliver, hearth and bellows in a smith's shop, Dudley Museum

25 Nailmaking on the oliver in Dudley Museum

palms of his hands which are brought together so that the fingers on one side point towards the wrist on the other; the ends of the wires are then pressed upon the grindstone, and by a slight motion of the hands to and fro, each wire is made to turn upon its axis at the same time, and thus they are all pointed perfectly.[10]

Pointing was followed by tempering and this was done by heating the needles on a charcoal fire until they became red hot. They were then thrown into cold water. Again they were heated, but since most of the needles would be crooked, they had to be straightened by hand, using an anvil and small hammer. Finally, needles were scoured and heaps of needles were placed on buckram sprinkled with emery dust and olive oil. The buckram, containing perhaps 20,000 needles, was rolled up, placed under the feet of a workman and scoured by moving the feet backward and forward as he sat at work at other processes. Alternatively, scouring could be done at the bench, after which the needles were washed in soap and water. Finally the needles were placed in a container containing moist bran. The container was hung in the workshop and the needles removed for pack ing when the bran was perfectly dry. These hand methods wer those that persisted in the Redditch district until about 1830, b they persisted even later since many of the hand-workers were t old to learn the new way of making needles.

From about 1830 to the end of the nineteenth century, the hand methods of needle production gave way to factory meth although outwork continued on a limited scale long after the in duction of power-driven machinery. In the early factories, wire cut into lengths required for the needles; the metal was then he and pointed at both ends. The eyes were bored with a stam machine, filed, cut and scoured by machinery. Division of labou usual in early factories, and the principal workers concerned

1. *The cutter*, operating a guillotine to cut wire to the correc

2. *The rubber* concerned with straightening the wires by r and rolling heated wires with a slightly curved iron bar ca rubbing file'.

3. *The pointer* concerned with grinding points on needles.

4. *The stamper* who shapes the head and pierces the eyes of A good stamper was said to be capable of stamping 30,000

day. Stamping 'not only fashions the head, makes the little groove below the eye to carry the thread, but also beats the eye almost through, so that there is only a thin film of steel to be punched out'.[11]

5. *The eyer*, concerned with punching out the eyes with a hand-operated press. Women and children were mainly employed in this task.

6. *The filer* whose task it was to cut the pairs of stamped needles into single needles and finally trim them with a file.

7. *The hardener*, considered a highly skilled craftsman, concerned with tempering needles by heating them and then plunging them in cold water or oil. The needles were then reheated.

8. *The scourer*. To scour needles, the technique was to 'cut coarse hempen cloth, called "hurden", into strips, lay them in a wooden trough some score inches long . . . pour in oil . . . and powdered quartz, then some soft soap spread along the top'. The needles were

Fig. 8 Rolls of needles ready for scouring

22 A fork forge at Abbeydale Industrial Hamlet, Sheffield

23 Tilt hammers at Abbeydale

then formed into rolls, tied firmly with string and rubbed constantly on a wooden 'runner bench'. The rubbing action of one needle against the other and with powdered quartz, soap and oil added, provided a glistening needle, but the rolls were often re-made with finer powder and fresh soap at regular intervals; the last scouring being with 'polishing putty' (oxide of tin). After perhaps ten days of scouring, the needles were boiled in water and dried in sawdust. The scourer then passed them through a sieve and sorted the damaged ones from the good. Up to 70,000 needles could be accommodated in one run.

9. *The hander*, concerned with the final sorting of the needles according to size and quality, each grade being known as a 'handing'. The needles were then weighed into small packets of a thousand each.

10. *The finisher* concerned with 'drilling'—the scouring away of all traces of burr by using a rapidly revolving drill; 'blue pointing'—the last polishing of the shank of the needle on an emery-dressed buffer; 'grinding' and 'setting' being the final smoothing of the head and point.

By the end of the nineteenth century all these processes of needle manufacture had become highly mechanised, although the basic processes were similar to those of earlier years. A great variety of needles were and are made by Redditch manufacturers, ranging from 'sharps' for ordinary sewing purposes to sewing machine needles and from sail needles to those used in stocking frames. Closely allied to the trade of needle-making is that of making fish hooks and Redditch has long been the centre, not only for hooks, but for other fishing equipment as well.

CHAPTER THIRTEEN

Nails and Chains

Two craft industries that had their origin in widely distributed cottage workshops in the Black Country were nail-making and chain-making by hand. While nail-making ceased to be a domestic industry early in the present century, chain-making by hand still persists in small backyard workshops in the Cradley Heath and Quarry Bank districts, although there is every likelihood that the next few years will see the end of this once important craft industry.

Nails

The craft of making nails by hand is one of great antiquity and was well known in ancient Israel as well as in Roman times. Nail-making in more recent centuries in Britain was regarded as an essential task for every country blacksmith. A variety of nails ranging from strake nails, used for fastening sections of metal bands to wooden vessels to small slate nails, boot and clog nails, were made at most smithies. Strake nails were large, blunt and tapered, and were equipped with large square heads. They were made by hand and usually required the services of two men. A rod of iron was heated and hammered to the required shape on the anvil. In the anvil orifice a cutting tool called a hardy was inserted, and the rod was cut to the required length on this tool. Each one was then heated again and inserted in a nail heading tool which consisted of a flat metal bar fitted at one or both ends with a deep perforated knob; the perforation was also countersunk to correspond with the nail head. After inserting the metal rod in the nail hole, the tool was placed over the anvil orifice and the head hammered into shape. The process of making nails in most country smithies was similar to that of making strake nails, but their tips could be either filed or hammered to a point. When hammering of nail points was carried out, the usual process was to place each nail in turn on a metal square fitted to a pointing horse. The craftsman sat astride this and then a hammer pointed each nail.

In addition to nails made by hosts of country blacksmiths for their own use or for use in the locality of the workshop, nail-making on a very large scale developed in the West Midlands of England. The stronghold of the industry since the early seventeenth century has been the Black Country, and nail-making was practised not only in such towns as Birmingham, Dudley and Wolverhampton, but also in the villages and small towns of the area. Until the last quarter of the nineteenth century nail-making was a widely distributed cottage industry, carried out in small workshops, many of them improvised lean-to sheds. Most of the workshops accommodated one or two nailers, but some had half a dozen or so heaters and the other simple equipment required in the industry. The main piece of equipment required was a foot-powered hammer called 'an oliver'. In principle this operated like a pole lathe, the hammer being connected to a springy ash, larch or birch pole, firmly fixed to the ground. By pressing the foot treadle the oliver would fall with considerable force on the metal placed on the bench beneath, but spring back by the action of the pole as soon as the foot was removed from the treadle. A nailer working at the block or anvil could have two hammers with two sets of poles close together. The wrought iron used in the nail-making industry, until it was superseded by steel in the latter half of the nineteenth century, was heated in the hearth on the lefthand side of the nailer and then transferred for shaping on the block in front of the craftsman. The earliest form of block was made of stone[1], with a series of metal shaping devices, known as setts, on the surface. Later the block, an iron slab anvil with a variety of setts attached, was the usual device in use. The iron setts were often made by the nailers themselves and varied considerably, according to the shape and size of nails being made. For example, to produce flat faces on nails, flat block setts were required, while for nail heads a holed sett was inserted in the block orifice, while every block had to be equipped with a cutting sett, for cutting off lengths of nail rod. Small flatfaced hand hammers and small tongs for handling shaped nails were also essential pieces of equipment. One of the most important technical innovations in the hand nail-making industry was the slitting mill, in which hammered pieces of wrought iron were cut into narrow rods, patented as early as 1588. In the mill, cutter wheels mounted in sets on each of two shafts, one above the other, sheared the heated strips of iron passed through it. Slitting mills that supplied domestic nailers with raw material were to be found throughout the West Midlands.

In a domestic system of manufacture, such as was found in the Black Country, an essential person was the nail master responsible for supplying rod iron to the nailers and also for purchasing the completed nails. It is said that many of these nail merchants were unscrupulous and they became known as 'foggers'. Many found it easy to enter the nail trade, 'since very little capital outlay was required to set up in business, and also the majority of the poverty stricken and illiterate nailers were easy prey to their schemes'. The foggers in supplying bundles of nail rods to nailers often gave short measure and many were said to be dishonest. Payment was often made in tokens and the nailers were expected to buy all their food and other necessities in the truck shop owned by the nail merchant. In addition, 'some of the rod iron was inferior in quality and was incapable of being worked into sound quality nails. In such cases the nailer often had no redress, since the nail foggers were numerous and influential, making it difficult for him to take his trade elsewhere with any chance of improvement.'

The hand industry flourished until the beginning of the present century, although with the innovation of new power-driven machinery during the last half of the nineteenth century, much of it had become factory based. Drawn wire began to be used for nail-making about 1860 and this, combined with the heavy importation of cheap cut nails from other countries, contributed to a considerable depression among the nailers of the Black Country. By the early years of the twentieth century the characteristic backyard nail shops, where families were engaged in almost round-the-clock work, had largely disappeared, to be replaced by a factory industry.

Chains

One of the heaviest and most demanding of all craft industries is that of chain-making by hand; indeed in the half dozen or so chain-making shops in the Black Country, the demands of the craft are such that workers are only able to work in shifts of four hours at a time. At Quarry Bank and Cradley Heath, hand chain-making still persists, although there is every likelihood that the next five years will see the end of the craft. There are difficulties in obtaining the right grade of fuel for the hearths and difficulties in obtaining the right grade of Lancashire wrought iron, in rod form, which the chain makers have always preferred. Above all, there is great difficulty in obtaining labour, for few young men are prepared to enter an industry that is always demanding, and as the older chain makers retire there is no one to succeed them. Payment in chain-making is always on a piecework system, and the total number of hand workers is at present less than fifty, with the largest of the workshops employing no more than twelve craftsmen. Until fairly recent times the craft was practised both in factories and home chain shops in Halesowen, Old Hill, Mushroom Green, Netherton, Lye and Careless Green, as well as in Cradley and Quarry Bank.

Although metals such as silver and gold were used for making chains in antiquity, it was not until 1634 that a blacksmith named Philip White obtained a patent for making an iron mooring chain. Oddly enough the industry did not develop on any scale until the early nineteenth century when wrought iron of excellent quality had become increasingly available. Wrought iron has always been preferred to steel in chain making because of its anti-corrosion properties. By the end of the first quarter of the nineteenth century, many blacksmiths in the Midlands had become competent chain makers.

> To Thomas Bunton perhaps should be accorded the greatest credit, in that it was he who overcame one of the greatest obstacles— namely the tendency of iron to stretch under strain—by inventing a two piece link with a central stud. . . . Bunton's idea opened the way for others and in 1820 Noah Hingley forged the first ship's cable, carrying out this enterprising work in his little village smithy by means of a forge, hammer and anvil'.[2]

Very soon, chains had largely replaced manila ropes for mooring ships, and this was one of the factors that contributed to the decline of the heavy rope making industry in Dorset and the specialisation of Bridport craftsmen in making nets, sails and twine rather than thick naval mooring ropes. Chain-making in iron producing districts, especially the Midlands, became an increasingly important industry and blacksmiths who had hitherto spread their activities over a wide field became specialist chain makers. Village chain shops became commonplace and the making of the lighter varieties of chain was often carried out by women in their cottage homes. Chain-making, as a craft unlike many other industries, did not have its origins in antiquity but developed during the early nineteenth century, and it is surprising that it should have developed in such a primitive fashion, when one would have thought that it would have developed along modern industrial lines. Nevertheless despite its late foundation, it developed as a handicraft with its domestic aspects of manufacture and with a development from small country blacksmiths' shops, where specialisation in chains only began in a late period.

In a typical chain shop such as that still operated at Noah Bloomer's Chain Works at Cradley Heath, the outstanding feature are the hearths around a central courtyard where the chain is made. Each one is manned by two or more chain-makers, dressed in rough canvas aprons held up by leather belts, the canvas is roughly cut-up tarpaulin and is not machined round the edges. Some wear patched flannel shirts, reinforced with a cloth square on the chest to prevent burning the skin. A towel hangs near the hearth and is continuously used as a sweat cloth, while bottles of water drunk at frequent intervals are an essential part of the equipment of each smith. For a heavy gauge chain such as that used for anchors, which may be $1\frac{1}{2}$ inches in diameter, a team of strikers is required. The smith himself holds the work and as many as three strikers deliver the blows by heavy hammers and sledges. In the manufacture of very heavy chains, it was customary to use very heavy hammers, with several shafts to a single head, operated by several men at once.

The rod iron, after delivery to the workshop, is cut up into lengths on a guillotine, and a coke fire is lit in the hearths. Until recently spale baskets which were widely made in the Wyre Forest[3] were used for transporting coke to the hearths, but now withy baskets are used. A 'scoven' or long-handled flat, metal shovel is used to push the coke down into the hearth. The hearth itself is made of brick and the blast is today electrically blown, although in the past the blast was supplied from a large hand-operated pear-shaped leather bellows on the left hand side of the hearth. This was operated either by a treadle or beam. Water circulates through the tue-iron down the feed pipe and back into the 'bosh' or tank through what is termed a throwing iron. The tremendous heat of the hearth would soon burn away the tue iron without some form of cooling.

The anvils used for chain-making vary according to the size of chain being made, and the tools used for shaping are in most cases not fixed to the anvil, but are spread out separately. This is specially the case with hearths where smaller chain is made. For example, there can be a separate hardy, not inserted in the anvil orifice, while the bending pegs may be set into the wall of the hearth and not in the anvil. Another piece of equipment, equivalent to the nail-maker's 'oliver' is a trip hammer known as a 'tommy'. This is operated by a treadle and is operated by one man to finish off the joints on the links of a chain. Formerly the spring was provided from a beam set over the anvil and suspended from the rafters, but nowadays two large extension springs are used.

The 'dolly' consists of a hinged tool fixed to this anvil and this is flipped over to finish off the join on the link, while the 'rag-chain' is a piece of chain used to balance the weight of the completed links. These are then fed to a large ring. The chain-maker also requires a metal handling hook, with a T-shaped metal handle and a variety of tongs. The principal types of tongs are holders, with hollow ends for grasping a piece of rod at right angles; hollow tongs for holding metal bars end on and benders with hooked jaws for bending the chain links around. Hammers of different weights are also required, and these are of a type that can be found in any blacksmith's shop, without particular names or specific designs for chain making.

To make a small gauge chain, a 'jump chain' of about half an inch in diameter, the links are joined as if jumped into each other sideways on and only slightly crossed. A long bar of small, light gauge rod is used and this is cut while red hot and shaped on the swage. It is then manipulated on the bender and the ends hammered together on the T-anvil or bick iron. Larger chain of $1\frac{1}{2}$ inches diameter, for example, is known as 'scarf chain', and the ends of each link are crossed over to a greater extent than in a jump chain. The cut pieces of rod iron are heated, using the holder tongs and the link is manipulated in the bender using the bender tongs. The links are then hammered and finished with a tommy. To strengthen this chain, metal studs are often inserted in the links while they are still hot.

The finished chain is tested for strength by a hydraulic apparatus on a chain testing bed. A chain maker's hook is used by the tester for dragging the chain, and if necessary it can be japanned or pitched before it is ready for sale.

Chain-making by hand is a craft that demands considerable strength, and many chainsmiths start work as early as 4.00 a.m. while others begin at 7.00 a.m. No chain-making is carried out in the afternoons, although most smiths, who are also responsible for paying strikers, fix their own hours of work and are paid a piecework rate.

References

1   J. G. Jenkins, *The English Farm Wagon* (Reading, 1961).
2   E. E. Evans, *Irish Folkways* (London, 1957), p. 135.
3   L. J. Mayes, *History of Chair Making in High Wycombe* (London, 1961).
4   H. E. Fitzrandolph and M. D. Hay, *Rural Industries of England and Wales*, vol. iii (Oxford, 1926), pp. 72–123.
5   C. E. Freeman, *Luton and the Hat Industry* (Luton, 1953).

CHAPTER TWO   *Ropes and Nets*

1   K. R. Gilbert, 'Rope making' in C. Singer, and others, eds., *A History of Technology*, vol. i (Oxford University Press, 1957), i, 451–4.
2   G. B. Hughes, *Living Crafts* (London, 1953), p. 81.
3   J. Claridge, *General View . . . of Agriculture . . . of Dorset* (London, 1795), p. 26.
4   J. Pahl, 'The rope and net industry of Bridport', in *Proceedings of the Dorset Natural History and Archaeological Society*, vol. lxxxii (1960), p. 144.
5   Fitzrandolph and Hay, 198.
6   E. W. Brayley, and J. Britton, *Beauties of England and Wales* (1801), vol. iv, p. 519.
7   Fitzrandolph and Hay, 200.
8   Dursley, Gloucestershire, was an important centre of rope making, for, in addition to the old rope yard established in 1600, there were also about a dozen other rope-makers in production in the 1920s.
9   Abraham Rees, *New Cyclopaedia of Arts and Sciences* (1819), vol. xxx.

CHAPTER THREE   *Straw Plait and Rush Mats*

1   Freeman, *Luton and the Hat Industry*, p. 13.
2   *Ibid.*, p. 13.
3   A. H. Dodd, *The Industrial Revolution in North Wales* (Cardiff, 1933), pp. 299–300.
4   O. Williamson, *Hanes Niwbwrch* (n.d.), p. 81.
5   *Cymru*, vol. xxxv (1908), p. 77.
6   A. M. Jones, *Rural Industries of England and Wales*, vol. iv (Oxford, 1927), p. 76.
7   *Ibid.*, p. 76.
8   Williamson, pp. 76–80.
9   Jones, p. 27.
10 Williamson, p. 80.

CHAPTER FOUR   *Paper*

1   Hughes, *Living Crafts*, p. 129.
2   A. Rees, *Cyclopaedia . . . of Arts, Sciences and Literature* (1819) vol. xxvi.
3   D. Diderot, *Pictorial Cyclopaedia of Trade and Industry* (1959 ed.) p. 363.
4   *Ibid.*
5   J. Overton, 'A note on technical advances in the manufacture of paper', in C. Singer and others, eds., *A History of Technology*, vol. iii (Oxford, 1957), p. 411.

CHAPTER FIVE   *Pottery*

1   C. Sempill, 'English pottery and porcelain' in W. J. Turner, ed., *British Craftsmanship* (London, 1947), p. 157.
2   P. C. D. Brears, *The English Country Pottery* (Newton Abbot, 1971), p. 40.
3   *Ibid.*, p. 41.
4   Sempill, p. 172.
5   Brears, p. 88.
6   *Ibid.*, p. 125.

Gazetteer

A number of craft industries have been preserved in museums in Britain. At the Welsh Folk Museum, St Fagan's, near Cardiff, a tannery from the Radnorshire town of Rhaeadr has been re-erected. In this building tanning was carried out in a series of over fifty oak-lined tan pits and the craft of the currier as well as the tanner is represented. The Rhaeadr tannery in its original setting employed a dozen men and was located on the banks of Cae Siams Brook within half a mile of the market town of Rhaeadr. Until 1860 the currier's shop was not a part of the tannery and tanners and curriers were separate craftsmen with their own premises. At the Welsh Folk Museum too the equipment of many other craft industries, such as clog and boot making, pottery and basket making, are represented, but as yet not all the collections are on exhibition. It is hoped that a new building for the display of craft material will be ready within the next four years.

Although the Department of Industry at the National Museum of Wales in Cardiff is mainly concerned with the heavier type of industry, there are important items of craft material on exhibition: the most interesting being a tilt hammer used for shovel making at a Cardiganshire forge.

Midland museums, such as the Dudley Museum and the Birmingham Museum of Science and Industry, have important collections of material relating to the small industrial undertakings of the Black Country. Northampton Museum has a unique collection of boots and shoes and a comprehensive collection of material relating to the industry, as has the new Industrial Museum in Leicester. The chair-making industry is well represented by the Borough Museum, High Wycombe and the private collection of chairs at Messrs Parker Knoll's premises in High Wycombe is well worth a visit.

Among the museums that have valuable collections of craft material are the Ulster Folk Museum at Cultra Manor, Holywood, Co. Down, where a tilt hammer may be seen at work in shovel making. Beamish Open-air Museum at Stanley, Co. Durham, which when developed will have an excellent collection of North of England industrial material, and Abbeydale industrial hamlet in Sheffield is unique. The best collection of baskets may be seen at the Museum of English Rural Life in the University of Reading, and for glass-making, the superb Pilkington Museum at St Helens should be visited.

The following is a list of the more important museums possessing craft material:

Alton, Hampshire—Curtis Museum (collections of rural craft material such as rake making and besom making).
Beamish, Co. Durham—North of England Open-air Museum.
Belfast—Ulster Folk Museum, Holywood.
Birmingham—Museum of Science and Industry.
Birmingham—Sarehole in Museum, Hall Green.
Bolton—Textile Machinery Museum.
Bradford—Industrial Museum.
Bridport—Museum and Art Gallery (Net making equipment especially).
Cardiff—National Museum of Wales, Department of Industry.
Cardiff—Welsh Folk Museum, St Fagans.
Coventry—Herbert Art Gallery and Museum.
Derby—Royal Crown Derby Museum.
Dudley—Museum and Art Gallery and Black Country Museum (in preparation).
Edinburgh—Royal Scottish Museum, Department of Technology.
Edinburgh—National Museum of Antiquities of Scotland.
Halifax—Bankfield Museum and Shibden Hall.
Hartlebury—Worcestershire County Museum.
High Wycombe—Museum and Art Gallery.
Honiton—Museum (especially lace making).
Kendal—Abbot Hall Museum of Lakeland Life and Industry.
Leeds—Kirkstall Abbey House Museum.
Leicester—Newarke Houses Museum.
Leicester—Industrial Museum (in preparation).
Lincoln—Museum of Lincolnshire Life.
Liverpool—City Museum.
London—Science Museum.
London—Geffrye Museum.

26 Welding on the tommy or 'oliver' in the nail trade

27 Hand chain making shop at Mushroom Green *c.* 1880

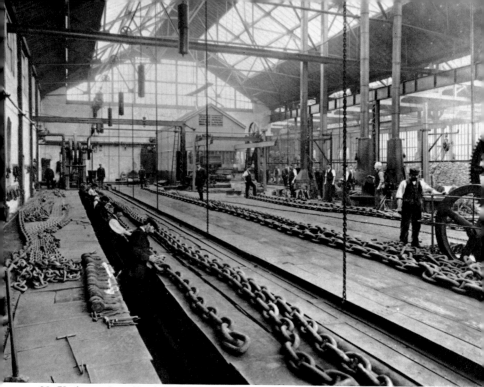

28 Chain testing. Each link is inspected and tested for strength

29 Hand forging a coupling approximately 6″ in diameter

London—London Museum.

Luton—Museum and Art Gallery (lacemaking and straw plaiting especially).

Newcastle upon Tyne—Museum of Science and Engineering.

Northampton—Museum and Art Gallery.

Norwich—Bridewell Museum of Local Industries & Rural Crafts.

Nottingham—Industrial Museum.

Reading—Museum of English Rural Life, The University.

St Albans—City Museum (houses the R. A. Salaman collection of craft tools).

St Helens—Pilkington Glass Museum.

Sheffield—Abbeydale Industrial Hamlet.

Shugborough—Staffordshire County Museum.

Stoke Bruerne—Waterways Museum.

Stowmarket—Abbot Hall Museum of Rural Life of East Anglia.

Teeside—Dorman Museum.

Telford—Ironbridge Gorge Museum (in preparation).

Walsall—Museum of Leathercraft.

York—Castle Museum.

Not all working craft workshops welcome visitors, but a number are worth visiting. Basket-making can be seen in a number of workshops in the Athelney district of Somerset; many of the workshops having retail shops attached to them. Two working tanneries at Colyton, Devon, and Grampound, Cornwall, illustrate a craft that has not changed in essentials since prehistoric times, while rope and net making may be seen at Bridport, Dorset; Castleton, Derbyshire; and Hawes, Yorkshire. Potteries are commonplace, and in addition to those in Staffordshire, country potteries of considerable interest may be seen at Farnham, Surrey, and Ewenni, Glamorgan. Chain-making by hand can still be seen at Cradley Heath and Dudley, while Forge Mill, Redditch, which was used for needle-finishing for domestic craftsmen, has been preserved. Other workshops of considerable interest that have been preserved are the flint grinding mill providing ground flints for the pottery industry at Cheddleton near Leek, preserved by the Cheddleton Flint Mill Trust, and the Finch Foundry, Sticklepath, Okehampton, Devon. The latter is a complete water-powered edge tool making plant which worked from 1814 until 1960 and is now maintained by the Finch Foundry Trust.

Select Bibliography

ABELL, W. *The Shipwright's Trade*, Cambridge University Press, 1948.

BAKER, J. and LAMMER, A. *English Stained Glass*, London, Thames & Hudson, 1960.

BARKER, T. C. *Pilkington Brothers and the Glass Industry*, Allen & Unwin, 1960.

BEMROSE, G. *Nineteenth Century English Pottery and Porcelain*, London, Faber, 1952.

BOBART, H. *Basketry Through the Ages*, Oxford University Press, 1936.

Book of English Trades, 1827.

BREARS, P. C. D. *The English Country Pottery—its history and techniques*, Newton Abbot, David & Charles, 1971.

CALKIN, J. B., ed. *Modern Pulp and Paper Making*, London, Chapman & Hall, 1957.

CARNELL, H. A. *Leather*, London, Gill, 1950.

CLAPPERTON, R. H. and HENDERSON, W. *Modern Paper Making*, Oxford, Blackwell, 1952.

DONY, J. G. *A History of the Straw Hat Industry*, Luton, Gibbs and Bamforth & Co, 1942.

EDLIN, H. L. *Woodland Crafts in Britain*, London, Batsford, 1949.

Folk Life, Journal of the Society for Folk Life Studies, 1963 to date.

FREEMAN, C. *Luton and the Hat Industry*, Luton Museum, 1953.

GALE, W. K. V. *The Black Country Iron Industry: a technical history*, London, Iron and Steel Institute, 1966.

HAARER, A. E. *Ropes and Rope Making*, Oxford University Press (Men and Women at Work Series), 1958.

HINSWORTH, J. B. *The Story of Cutlery* (1923).

HONEY, W. B. *English Pottery and Porcelain*, rev. by R. J. Charleston, London, A. and C. Black, 1962.

HUGHES, G. B. *Living Crafts*, London, Lutterworth Press, 1953.

HUGHES, G. B. *Victorian Pottery and Porcelain*, London, Country Life, 1959.

HUNTER, D. *Paper Making: the history and technique of an ancient craft*, London, Pleiades, 1948.

JENKINS, J. G. *Traditional Country Craftsmen*, London, Routledge, 1965.

KENYON, G. H. *The Glass History of the Weald*, Leicester University Press, 1967.

LABARRE, E. J. *Dictionary and Encyclopaedia of Paper and Paper Making*, Oxford University Press, 1952.

LLOYD, G. I. H. *The Cutlery Trade*, 1913.

Medieval Archaeology, 1956 to date.

MOXON, JOSEPH. *Mechanick exercises or the doctrine of handy works*, 1703.

NORRIS, F. H. *Paper and Paper Making*, Oxford University Press, 1952.

OKEY, THOMAS. *An Introduction to the Art of Basket Making*, 1912.

OXFORD UNIVERSITY AGRICULTURAL ECONOMICS RESEARCH INSTITUTE. *The Rural Industries of England and Wales*, 4 vols., 1926–7.

Post Medieval Archaeology, 1967 to date.

PROCTOR, H. R. *The Making of Leather*, 1914.

RACKHAM, B. and RHEAD, H. *English Pottery*, 1924.

SANDFORD, L. and DAVIS, P. *Decorative Straw Work*, London, Batsford, 1964.

SALZMAN, L. F. *English Industries in the Middle Ages*, 1913.

SCHRIJVER, ELKA. *Glass and Crystal*, 2 vols., London, Merlin Press, 1963–4.

SHAW, J. T. *The Potteries of Sunderland and District*, Sunderland Museum, 1961.

SHAW, SIMEON. *History of the Staffordshire Potteries* (1829) Newton Abbot, David & Charles, 1971.

SINGER, C. J. and others, eds.: *A History of Technology*, 5 vols., Oxford University Press, 1954–58.

SMITH, DONALD. *Metalwork: an introductory historical survey* (1948), London, Batsford 1956, 2nd edn.

STANDAGE, H. C. *The Leather Worker's Manual*, 1920.

THORNTON, J. H., ed. *Textbook of Footwear Manufacture*, 2nd edn., London, National Trade Press, 1959.

TOMLINSON, C. *Illustrations of Useful Arts, Manufacture and Trades* (1858).

TYLECOTE, R. F. *Metallurgy in Archaeology*, London, E. Arnold, 1962.

URE. *Dictionary of Arts Manufacture and Mines*, 4 vols., 1878.

WEDGWOOD, J. C. and ORMSBEE, T. H., *Staffordshire Pottery*, rev. edn., London, Putnam, 1947.

WOODS, K. S. *Rural Crafts of England*, London, Harrap, 1949.

WRIGHT, DOROTHY. *Baskets and Basketry*, London, Batsford, 1959.

WYMER, N. *English Town Crafts*, London, Batsford, 1949.

Index